Damn Senators

My Grandfather and the Story of Washington's Only World Series Championship

Mark Gauvreau Judge

ENCOUNTER BOOKS
SAN FRANCISCO, CALIFORNIA

First edition published in 2003 by Encounter Books, an activity of Encounter for Culture and Education, Inc., a nonprofit tax exempt corporation.

Encounter Books website address: www.encounterbooks.com
Manufactured in the United States and printed on acid-free paper.

The paper used in this publication meets the minimum requirements of ANSI/NISO Z39.48-1992 (R 1997)(*Permanence of Paper*).

Library of Congress Cataloging-in-Publication Data

Judge, Mark Gauvreau.
    Damn senators : my grandfather and the story of Washington's only World Series championship / Mark Gauvreau Judge.
        p.   cm.
    Includes bibliographical references and index.
    ISBN 1-59403-045-6
    1. Judge, Joe, 1894–1963.   2. Washington Senators (Baseball team)—History.   3. World Series (Baseball) (1924).   4. Baseball players—United States—Biography.   I. Title.
GV875.W3 J83 2003
796.357'64'09753—dc21

                                                                2003040858

                    10 9 8 7 6 5 4 3 2

Jacket photo of Joe Judge from a baseball card.

All interior photos are in the public domain and courtesy of the Library of Congress except the photo of Babe Ruth knocked out—courtesy of Culver Pictures, and the photo of Johnson and Judge on Joe Judge Day—courtesy of Transcendental Graphics.

To Aunt Dorothy

Contents

Preface

REMEMBRANCE OF BASEBALL PAST

From where I was standing at Washington's Robert Francis Kennedy Stadium, it was hard to see my father, surrounded as he was by officials on the fifty-yard line. My mother and I and our relatives were stuck behind the end zone.

It was October 21, 1990, and my grandfather, Joe Judge, was being inducted into the stadium's Ring of Stars, a local hall of fame for Washington, D.C., athletes. Along with three other Washington greats—Redskins Joe Theisman and John Riggins, and former Washington Bullet Elvin Hayes—the name of Joe Judge was about to be added to a circle of names around the inner part of the stadium. The other inductees were there in person, but my grandfather had died in 1963, the year before I was born, and my father was representing him at the halftime ceremony. While I couldn't see Dad from where I stood in the bitter cold, I could hear RFK's public address announcer, as well as the anticipatory hum of the 55,000 fans in the stadium.

Washington has a reputation as city of transients who don't develop any attachment to the place; but that wasn't the town I knew. The city I grew up in was a place of local bars and rock bands, row houses, parks, rivers, diners and jazz clubs. And sports fans. Lots of them.

Indeed, Washington is a sports town with a long memory. It is also a place with baseball in its soul. The city has lost two versions of the Senators, one in 1960 and the other in 1971—

1

two seasons of heartbreak. So today, bereft of a team, many fans make the trip down the Beltway to Baltimore; it is estimated that as many as a third of the Orioles fans come from Washington. But it's not the same.

The RFK announcer read my grandfather's statistics—his 19 years in major league baseball from 1915 to 1934, all but the last two spent in Washington; a .298 batting average; 2,352 hits; 433 doubles; 1,037 RBIs; 1500 double plays; 1,284 assists; a .993 fielding average, which was the standard for first basemen for 30 years; his leadership of the American League in fielding percentage six times—and the crowd began to cheer. When the announcer mentioned that Joe Judge had been part of the 1924 team, the only Washington Senators squad to win a World Series, the cheering swelled to a roar.

For our family, it was a moment of vindication. Joe Judge was one of the greatest baseball players of all time, yet today he is largely forgotten. He was not the kind of player, or the kind of man, who drew a lot of attention to himself. He exemplified virtues that seem in short supply today, both in athletics and in our larger culture. Family, friends, sportswriters all describe him the same way: polite, taciturn, unassuming. Baseball writer Huck Finnegan put it more elegantly when he called Granddad "intelligent, courageous, personable, industrious and sober." A 1925 article in *Baseball* magazine emphasized his steadiness when it called him "the sheet anchor of the Washington infield."

Relatives, players who knew him, journalists, everyone he came in contact with describes him in the same way: as a man who could not be ruffled. He coached at Georgetown University after he retired, and one of his former players once recalled that the most upset he had ever seen Joe get was when he bumped into a group of his players in a bar after a particularly embarrassing loss. "That was baseball that could bring tears to the eyes of a hobbyhorse," he said with evident emotion.

My aunt Dorothy (Joe's daughter) had another telling story. Joe was at the house in Chevy Chase, Maryland, where he moved in the early 1930s. Busying himself for some guests in the kitchen, he dropped a bottle of milk. There was a loud crash of breaking glass. The visitors braced themselves for the vulgar tirade for which baseball players were notorious. But from the kitchen came more restrained sounds of complaint: "Oh dear, oh dear, oh dear . . ."

Yet Joe Judge was a man sometimes capable of mischief and even, on very rare occasions, angry eruptions—at least on the diamond. Somewhat reclusive off the field, he could come alive as a moral presence in this intensely competitive team sport. In 1928, the Senators slugger Goose Goslin was leading the league in hitting. On the last day of the season, he was just a fraction of a point ahead of Heinie Manush of the St. Louis Browns for the batting title. The Browns were in town for the last game, and when it came time for Goose's final turn at bat, Manush was at .378 and he was at .379. Senators manager Bucky Harris let Goose know that he didn't have to bat if he didn't want to. He decided not to. Then he heard a voice from the dugout.

"You better watch out," Joe Judge said, "or they'll call you yellow."

"What are you talking about?" Goose said.

Judge pointed to Heinie Manush in left field. "What do you think he'll figure if you win the title by sitting on the bench?"

Goslin batted, and after trying unsuccessfully to get thrown out of the game by arguing a pitch call, he got a hit and won the 1928 batting title fair and square.

After the announcer at RFK read off the statistics for all the Ring of Stars inductees, the tarpaulin covering their names was dropped.

Joe Judge was a star in Washington again. How he became one the first time, and helped bring a championship to his city, is one of the great stories in baseball.

BASEBALL AND THE CITY

Baseball had been a feature of Washington's civic life for more than fifty years before my grandfather arrived on the scene to play for the Senators. That was in 1915.

The game first came to the city in the summer of 1859, when a group of government clerks formed a team named the Potomacs. Later that year another local team, the Nationals, was organized. In the spring of 1860 the Potomacs challenged the Nationals to a game, which was played on a field behind the White House called the White Lot—the site of today's Ellipse. The Potomacs won the game, scoring 35 runs. (Accounts differ on how many runs the Nationals scored.) A newspaper reported that after the game, the teams "partook of rich entertainment prepared for them ... at the order of the Potomac Club"—in other words, they celebrated at a bar. The Potomac Club was then at the Ebbit Hotel, one block from the White House. And it's still there.

This vignette is a reminder that baseball was a middle-class recreation before farmers and immigrants (and their sons, in my grandfather's case) took over the game. Baseball had its origins in the British game of rounders and took shape in the 1840s, mainly in America's growing cities. It was played by men of middle-class professional standing—after all, laborers couldn't take the afternoons off. The game grew in popularity, and in 1860 the Excelsior Club of Brooklyn went on the first baseball tour, traveling through Pennsylvania, Maryland and Delaware, to play, as baseball historian John P. Ross tells us, "before large crowds that were already deeply informed about baseball." He notes that the new game "perfectly fit the contours of the country—it was fast, dynamic and uniquely American."

In the years after that first game between the Potomacs and the Nationals, baseball quickly caught on in Washington. By 1865, six thousand fans, including President Andrew Johnson, watched the Nationals play the Brooklyn Atlantics and the Philadelphia Athletics. (Until the 1950s the true name of the team was the Washington Nationals; "Senators" was a nickname used by so many people that almost everyone assumed it was official.)

On July 11, 1867, the Nationals went on the first western tour in baseball history. (The frontier was then still expanding, so most of the territory they covered was actually what we know today as the Midwest.) The team paid its own way and was joined by Henry Chadwick, an English immigrant and one of the first sportswriters in America. A few years earlier, in addition to his other contributions to our national sport, he had come up with an ingenious system for organizing on paper the events of a baseball game: the box score.

The Nationals dominated the tour, blasting Cincinnati 53 to 10, then beating local teams from St. Louis, Indianapolis and Louisville. In Chicago, they lost their first game to a 17-year-old pitcher named Albert Goodwill Spalding. At the time, Spalding was earning five dollars a week as a grocery clerk in Rockford, Illinois. His showing against Washington was so impressive that he was recruited by a man named Harry Wright who was putting together a team in Boston. A. G. Spalding would be the sole pitcher on Boston's roster in 1871, and gain a record of 20–10. In 1875 it would be 56–4. He would also go on to form his own sporting goods company, becoming one of the most successful sports entrepreneurs in American history.

The day after their defeat at the hand of Spalding, the Nationals trounced the Chicago Excelsiors, inducing the *Chicago Tribune* to accuse Washington of having thrown the game against Spalding so they could get better odds and clean up against Chicago. After a visit from Nationals president Frank Toner and player Arthur Gorman, the paper printed a retraction. Gorman would go on to become a U.S. senator; according to some, he was responsible for the "Senators" nickname.

Within three years, another Washington team had been formed, the Olympics. It was organized by Nicholas H. Young, who would later be credited with forming the National League of Professional Ballplayers. Young, who had learned to play baseball while fighting in the Civil War, was an outfielder for the Nationals, and ran a school for umpires in D.C. Along with the Olympics came other D.C. teams: the Capitals, the Empires, the Unions, the Jeffersons.

Baseball was rapidly developing a more organized structure. In 1869 the first professional team, the Cincinnati Red Stockings, was formed. The payroll added up to $9,300, and the fact that they were paid at all meant that players would be chosen for their skills, not whether they could get afternoons off. The game itself was also evolving: batters were learning to change their stances to avoid hitting fly balls, which had become easy outs thanks to improved fielding strategies; and while pitchers had previously tossed the ball underarm, merely trying to put it into play, by now they were throwing with vastly more force and cunning, eager to engage in aggressive duels with hitters in order to strong-arm outs at all costs.

In Washington, the Nationals had a new man leading the organization. Mike Scanlon had played baseball since joining the Union Army at age fifteen. At the war's end, he arrived in Washington nearly broke; by 1866 he was already able to buy a poolroom on Ninth and S Streets, just a few blocks north of the White House. But Scanlon was crazy for baseball, and his energy soon attracted the attention of the city's other enthusiasts: Frank Jones, president of the Nationals; Arthur Gorman, former player and future senator from Maryland; wealthy businessman Robert Hewit; and Nicholas Young, head of the Olympic Club. Scanlon began organizing games on the White Lot behind the White House, and by 1869 crowds averaged four thousand people. President Johnson had the Marine Band play at the Saturday games. His successor, Ulysses S. Grant, watched from the South Lawn of the White House.

While Scanlon was boosting baseball in D.C., in New York the game's owners, managers and players were also organizing professionally. At a 1871 meeting, the National Association of Baseball Players decided to form themselves into a league. The National League would have teams in nine cities: New York; Philadelphia; Boston; Troy, New York; Chicago; Cleveland; Fort Wayne, Indiana; Rockford, Illinois; and Washington, which would be represented by the short-lived Olympics (the Nationals not joining the league until the following year).

IN 1886 THE NATIONALS ACQUIRED a catcher named Cornelius McGillicuddy, who would later become famous as Connie Mack, a name he came up with to fit in a box score. The Nationals were now playing at the Swampoodle Grounds, a field near what is now Washington's Union Station. An 1888 photograph shows the team facing the Chicago White Stockings, and Mack is unmistakable behind the plate. He had an Ichabod Crane body, and even in a picture taken from a distance he stands out like a flamingo among starlings. Mack made his major league debut for Washington on October 7, 1886, hitting a single and a triple in a 12–3 win over Kansas City. Mack would go on to own and manage the Philadelphia Athletics for half a century. Always a distinctive figure, emerging from the dugout in a business suit, not a uniform, he won championships in 1902, 1905, 1910 and 1911, and did not retire until 1950.

Cornelius McGillicuddy's destiny was emblematic of a new chapter in American sports: the rise of the Irish. Historian John Ross has noted that the first two sports heroes in America in the 1880s, boxer John L. Sullivan and Mike "King" Kelly of the Chicago White Sox, were both Irish. Ross adds that the anti-Irish and anti-immigrant American Protective Society was at its peak at this time, and "sport served to ease the path to acceptance of an outside group by the larger society."

While visiting Washington, players in the 1880s often stayed at the Willard Hotel on Pennsylvania Avenue, just down the street from the Capitol. Because of the intense Washington heat, they kept chairs on the sidewalk in front of the hotel and lounged on them after or between games. Pedestrians would walk by and strike up conversations, even offering players cigars or plugs of tobacco. The players took to calling the street the "Boulevard of Base Ball." One of the visiting players was "King" Kelly.

Kelly was one of the smartest and most flamboyant baseball players of the early era, playing every position (but mostly outfield or catcher). He was an early version of Babe Ruth, dressing in finely tailored clothes, spending lavishly and cutting a charismatic figure on the town at night. Kelly once told his manager he had to miss practice because he was taking a Turkish bath, only to have it revealed later that he had been at the racetrack. Chicago manager Cap Anson once said that Kelly "had one enemy, that being himself." At a time when the game had only one umpire, Kelly was apt to cut corners when he ran the bases. And in one famous episode he leapt from the bench yelling "Kelly now substituting!" and ran out onto the field to catch a fly ball. A popular song, "Slide, Kelly, Slide!" was written for him.

When Kelly was lounging in front of the Willard Hotel one night, a passing fan asked why Washington could not win a pennant. Kelly pointed to the Treasury building across the street. "Because you are so damned busy making money in that place across the street that you don't give enough to the honest occupation of playing baseball right."

⚭

IN 1891, WHEN THE ROSTER of teams in the National League was still shifting, with some coming and others going, Washington entered what would become known as the Wagner era. A new Washington Nationals team was formed and owned by two cutthroat Philadelphia businessmen, the brothers George and J. Earl Wagner. As the legendary Washington sportswriter Shirley Povich put it, "For the next eight years the city's fans found themselves in the cold clutch of a pair of baseball brokers who talked big, spent little, pocketed nice profits, and pulled out before they were kicked out." By the eighth year of the Wagners' reign, no Washington team finished better than a tie for sixth place. To make matters worse, a depression hit the country after farm prices collapsed in the South and Midwest. The number of fans attending baseball games in the United States dropped 40 percent from 1889 to 1894.

In order to boost attendance, owners sought to make changes in the game. In 1893 they strengthened offense by increasing the distance from the plate to the pitcher's mound from 50 feet to 60 feet 6 inches, the standard today, thus giving batters more time to see the ball. But nothing was going to help the Nationals under the aegis of the Wagner brothers. They hired and fired managers at will, inevitably turning Washington fans against them. In 1893 they announced that three games against the Philadelphia Athletics scheduled for Washington would instead be played in Philadelphia, for the insulting reason that fans there would turn out in greater numbers. A *Sporting Life* magazine headline justifiably bellowed that this was "An Outrage on the Washington Public." The Wagners were fined $1,000 by baseball authorities.

On another occasion the owners had their manager doing double duty: he had to lead the team and simultaneously oversee the production of "The Texas Steer Show," a theatrical extravaganza the brothers were financing. Yet another cockamamie farce was having Tuesdays and Fridays, when the handsome player Win Mercer was scheduled to pitch, billed as "Ladies' Days." Unfortunately for the Wagners, Mercer suffered from bouts of depression and a lethal gambling addiction, and when he ran up a debt of $8,000 and had a disastrous day at the horse track in Oakland, California, he took his own life. The suicide note he left behind read, "A word to friends: beware of women and a game of chance."

Even if the Wagners had been more serious about the team, the players may not have been always ready to take the field. "What's the matter with the Washington Baseball Club?" the *Washington Post* demanded in 1896, and then proposed a euphemistic answer: team members were "indulging in the flowing bowl." Whatever the case, the Wagners went through four managers in 1898, and an epitaph for the dismal team was offered by the *Post* when the Nationals returned home from a western trip in which they went 1–11. "The Senators," the *Post* reported, "passed through their home town unmolested on their way to Boston."

In 1899 the team ended the season in ninth place. It was generally a season of poor performances and the league directors were talking of shrinking from twelve teams to eight. J. Earl Wagner began entertaining offers for the Nationals, even while insisting publicly that "Washington will be in the major leagues when Baltimore and Brooklyn are in the minors." At the winter meetings of the National League Board of Directors, his brother George was voted off the board. At a subsequent meeting on January 25, 1900, it was decided that Washington, Cleveland, Louisville and Baltimore would all be dropped from the league. The Wagners sold the team for approximately $40,000.

$\mathcal{O}$

WASHINGTON DID NOT HAVE TO wait long for another baseball team. In September 1900 in a Chicago bar there was a meeting between Clark Griffith, a pitcher for the Chicago Colts; Charles Comiskey, owner of the Colts; and businessman Byron Bancroft ("Ban") Johnson. Johnson was a 300-pound, implacable cigar smoker who, as one reporter claimed, looked as though he had been "weaned on an icicle." Icicle or not, he had a passion for baseball, which he had played in college; but his real gifts were as a businessman. In 1894 he had taken over a struggling enterprise called the Western League and turned it into a success.

Ban Johnson found himself under pressure to abide by an agreement that his expanding Western League—now called the American League—could not raid players from the established National League, which was allowed to raid players from his own teams merely by plunking down $500 for any one of them. Johnson balked at such an inequitable deal, demanding that at least raids be kept down to two players per team and that the American League could expand into cities vacated by the National League.

National League officials retorted that Ban Johnson could "wait until hell freezes over" before they would agree to such a proposal. Johnson, whose hero was the poet laureate of the self-made man, Horatio Alger, took matters into his own hands and arranged a summit meeting with Charles Comiskey and Clark Griffith, who was not only a great pitcher but also the vice-president of the Ball Players Protective Association.

Griffith, who would become the legendary "Moses of Washington baseball," was born in 1869 and grew up poor in Vernon County, an outpost in western Missouri. His family lived in a log cabin until Clark's father was killed in a hunting accident in 1872—this when his mother, Sarah, was pregnant with her fifth child. Griffith learned to hunt and trap animals to help his family survive. When he was twelve he was diagnosed with "malarial fever," so the family moved to the healthier climate of Bloomington, Illinois. It was there that Clark met Charles "Old Hoss" Radbourne, one of the great pitchers of the day. Clark was tutored by this expert, and by age sixteen was making money playing baseball. In 1888 he signed his first professional contract for $225 a month with the Bloomington club of the Interstate League. He was then sold to a Milwaukee team, where he went 27–7 in 1890.

Griffith spent the next few years playing for different teams and leagues that formed and folded quickly. In 1893 he and a teammate, Joe Cantillon, spent time in San Francisco's notorious Barbary Coast district, working vaudeville skits in a honkytonk. (Cantillon would go on to manage the Senators, and would be the man responsible for signing Walter Johnson.) In these burlesques, Griffith was the Indian gunned down by a cowboy, played by his partner.

In 1893 James Hart, who had managed Griffith in Milwaukee and had become the president of the newly formed Chicago Colts of the National League, heard that he was available. He wired the pitcher to come to Chicago and serve as player-manager for the Colts. The Colts were owned by A. G. Spalding, the legendary pitcher who had smoked the Washington club on its road trip years before, and managed by the equally renowned Cap Anson. The first superstar in major league baseball, Anson was a handsome right-hander who stood just over six feet tall and sported a handlebar moustache. He had come to the Colts in 1876, hitting .343 and playing on the first National League championship team. It was said that Anson's reflexes were so quick he never got hit by a pitch. He played outfield and second base before settling in at first in 1879. He won four batting championships, and led the Colts to pennants in 1880, 1881, 1882, 1885 and 1886.

Griffith would win over twenty games in six straight seasons for Anson and the Colts. He was also, or so he claimed, the inventor of the screwball. In 1894, finding that his arm was growing sore, he started to experiment with different grips in the hope that he could come up with a slower pitch that would fool batters; he found one that made pitches sink away from left-handed batters.

Griffith was still twenty-five when he got his nickname, "the Old Fox," a tribute to his cunning as a pitcher. Although he was only 5'6", he knew individual batters and threw to their weaknesses. He tampered with the ball (this was still legal), rubbing it with tobacco and licorice—even a nail file—to produce unusual effects. Griffith was wily and talkative—some said obnoxious—and could annoy batters into striking out. The *Boston Post* once summed him up this way:

> We have seen Griffith pitching for the old Chicago Club and what a pesky individual he was to opponents, hostile grounds and umpires. All he seemed to have was a slow ball, a prayer and control, yet he makes monkeys out of the men who face him.

Griffith would stall endlessly between pitches just to drive the other team into a frenzy, and if that failed he would wrangle with umpires or taunt batters mercilessly. As one reporter dryly commented, "he won more games with his head than his arm."

C

AS A RESULT OF THEIR barroom meeting, Griffith, Ban Johnson and Charles Comiskey decided to create the American League. As vice-president of the Ball Players Protective Association, Griffith had access to players and their trust, and in the 1900 off season he traveled to various teams convincing players that his new league could give them a better deal than the National

League. He promised higher salaries, and by the end of his tour he had signed forty new players. The one person who wouldn't sign was a shortstop named Honus Wagner.

In 1901, Johnson sent the 31-year-old Griffith to New York for a meeting with representatives of the National League. Griffith carried with him a petition from the National League players demanding that they be allowed to play in the new league. Upon entering the owners' headquarters Griffith felt a tug on his sleeve. Turning, he came face to face with Nicholas Young, president of the National League. "Son," Young said, "they ain't gonna give you anything in this meeting. I just wanted to tell you."

Griffith spoke his piece, reciting complaints from players and handing National League vice-president A. H. Soden a petition. Soden assured Griffith that he would give the petition to the other owners.

Griffith retired to the bar in the basement of the hotel. By now players had gathered in the lobby, anxious for news. Griffith ordered a beer, then noticed someone coming down the stairs. It was A. H. Soden, trying to avoid the players in the lobby. Griffith, seeing the humor of the situation, invited him over for a beer. As Soden reached for his mug, Griffith noticed something in his pocket: the petition he had just delivered. The vice-president hadn't passed it on to the owners as he had promised. Griffith called him a liar, and Soden headed for the exit.

Griffith immediately went to the Associated Press and reported what had happened. Then he told players not to sign new contracts with National League teams. Ban Johnson started lining up backers for his new league, and declared that any previous agreements with the National League were null and void. In support, Ben and Tom Shibe, the Philadelphia sports goods manufacturers, got behind a team they called the Athletics. Charles Comiskey created a new team in Chicago called the White Sox and made Griffith the first manager. In the end, the league would consist of eight teams: Cleveland, Chicago, Detroit and Milwaukee (shifted to St. Louis after a year) from the old Western League, and four new teams—Baltimore, Boston, Philadelphia and Washington, D.C. Ban Johnson, president of the new league, would have controlling interest in the Senators.

The American League was an immediate hit, out-drawing the National League in its first year. The pennant was won by the White Sox, led by the 24–7 record of Clark Griffith. Washington was less fortunate, beginning a dismal run that would keep them from finishing any better than sixth place over the next ten years. They would also lose one of their best players, and one of the most flamboyant figures in the history of baseball, Ed Delahanty.

When Washington had signed him in 1902, "Big Ed" had been a feared hitter and brilliant outfielder for Philadelphia who had hit over .400 twice. He was a handsome, well-built fellow with a powerful jaw who led the National League in slugging in four of his eleven years with them. Playing in the "dead-ball era" when trick pitches were legal and the ball was filthy with saliva, licorice and tobacco and cut and scuffed past all recognition by the fifth inning, Delahanty used his terrific power to turn the tables on the pitchers. He went after the ball, not waiting patiently for his pitch like players today; Pat Tebeau, the manager of the Cleveland Spiders while Delahanty was there, once said that the worst thing you could do was throw Delahanty a wild pitch, because the big man just loved blasting those out of the park.

Delahanty had barely signed with Washington when he got an offer from the New York Giants of the rival National League. The offer came from manager John McGraw, who would lead the Giants against Washington in the 1924 World Series. McGraw was a brilliant player and manager, already a legend. Brazen, temperamental, sometimes eloquent and often violent, he was a force of nature for whom baseball was not only a livelihood but a life.

When McGraw was twelve his mother and four siblings succumbed to diphtheria. In his struggle to survive, he turned to baseball, and in 1891 was signed by the Baltimore Orioles and soon became notorious for his temper and his toughness. He was known as "Little Napoleon," and one writer summed him up this way: "If the bitter will to win could be rolled into one bundle and set on legs, it would probably have to look like the Little Napoleon from Truxton, New York." When McGraw was playing in Baltimore, a local writer described him as "the most loved man in town and the most hated everywhere else in the country." Another noted, "McGraw is a rattling good third baseman, but some [*sic*] of these mornings he will turn up missing. He will turn to give the wrong man the shoulder and somebody will drop."

This last was a prescient comment. In July 1913 the Giants were playing the Phillies when McGraw started to razz Phillies pitcher Ad Brennan. Brennan wasn't even playing until the next day, but McGraw wanted to rattle him early. He kept calling Brennan "yellow," continuing even after the game as the two men left the stadium. McGraw was walking behind Brennan when the pitcher suddenly wheeled around and punched him, knocking McGraw down and out.

Yet despite his raw pugnacity, McGraw was actually quite refined. He had attended college at St. Bonaventure, and spent almost as much time with writers and actors as he did at the track. People hated him or loved him, but all agreed that he was a baseball genius. As a player he led Baltimore to three pennants in the 1890s and went on to manage the Giants for thirty years, bringing the team ten pennants and three World Series.

The attempt to lasso Delahanty particularly irked Clark Griffith, who had a long history of face-offs with McGraw. As a player, the Little Napoleon once fouled off fifteen consecutive pitches from Griffith. Another time McGraw, crowding the plate while facing Griffith, was hit in the leg by a pitch, but umpire Hank O'Day called a strike. Griffith hit him with the next pitch, again in the knee. Strike two. McGraw didn't budge, and was hit again. Strike three. Griffith often said that his opponent had a "reputation beyond his ability." When McGraw died years later, his old rival told Shirley Povich of the *Washington Post,* "It is a great loss to baseball." Then, under his breath he whispered, "but McGraw was still an overrated player."

In 1900 McGraw was chosen by Ban Johnson to manage the new American League's Baltimore Orioles. He accepted, but was soon causing trouble. In 1902 Ban Johnson suspended McGraw for umpire-baiting. McGraw, who couldn't stand the way Johnson defended umpires, jumped to the National League and the New York Giants, who purchased his release for $100,000. So, on top of everything else, Clark Griffith always considered McGraw as the man who had sold out the American League. The two men would settle the score in the 1924 World Series.

McGraw's audacious effort to steal Delahanty from Washington didn't work. In 1903, leaders of the National League, sensing that the successful American League was a fact of life, made peace and agreed to work together. As a result, Delahanty was ordered to stay with Washington.

On Opening Day 1903, the players were taken in an open carriage to National Park, also known as League Park, a new diamond on Fourteenth Street and Bladensburg Road not far from Capitol Hill. The park announcer, E. Lawrence Phillips, gave the opening lineups by megaphone, a practice he had started the year before.

The players were then led by a marching band to home plate. The Senators' opponents were the Highlanders, a new American League team from New York. It was the very first game ever played by the Highlanders, who would eventually change their name to the Yankees. The team's pitcher, "Happy Jack" Chesbro, would win an astonishing 41 games in 1904—still a record. But on this occasion the Senators got the better of him, beating New York 3–1 before a crowd of 11,950. The hero of the game was Ed Delahanty, who drove in the winning run.

But despite this auspicious beginning, 1903 would be another terrible year for the Senators: they went 43–94 and finished last. They would also lose their star player in the middle of the season. Ed Delahanty was prone to excessive drinking and resulting bouts of despair, and on July 2, 1903, he boarded a train to upstate New York to visit his wife. He got drunk and began to misbehave, smoking in the sleeper car, ringing the car bell, breaking the glass case holding a firefighting ax, and then pulling at the bare ankles of a sleeping woman in the upper birth of a car. Near Bridgeburg, on the Canadian side of the Niagara River, Delahanty was kicked off the train. It was night, and he began crossing the International Bridge on foot. He never made it to the far side. He plunged into a ravine and died. A night guard testified to the smell of alcohol on his breath, but denied any physical contact. To this day, there is speculation about a scuffle on the bridge and what may have happened.

The Senators would finish in last place again in 1904, but would do so in a new location. It was called American League Park, and was one of the largest, oddest ball parks in the majors. The distances to left, center and right fields were 421–400–399, making it a home run hitter's nightmare. When the park went up, designers were frustrated by homeowners who refused to sell their properties located where far-right center field was planned to be, so they simply built the park around them, cutting the fence into a V in right center. Where the fence cut in there was a giant tree and a flagpole. Near the flagpole was an old doghouse where flags were stored. On one occasion the Senators were playing the Philadelphia Athletics when a Senator drove a ball over the head of center fielder Socks Seybold. The ball rolled into the doghouse, and when Seybold gave chase he got halfway into the house before getting stuck. It took three minutes to get him out, by which time the batter had scored on the only inside-the-doghouse home run ever recorded.

American League Park was ten blocks from the White House; in 1915 it was a fifteen-cent cab ride from door to door. It would be renamed Clark Griffith Stadium in 1923. Because the stadium is universally known to Washingtonians and sportswriters simply as Griffith Stadium, I will refer to it that way.

The new digs wouldn't help the team, who finished in seventh place in 1905 and 1906. Yet in 1907 fortune would smile when they were lucky enough to sign a gangly young pitcher named Walter Johnson, who would become one of the greatest pitchers in the history of the game.

WALTER JOHNSON WAS BORN IN 1887 on a farm in Allen County, Kansas, and his astounding ability was evident from an early age. When Johnson was a child he was playing a game of "One o' Cat," a type of baseball. When it came his turn to pitch, the older boys thought Johnson was too young. To prove them wrong, he hurled the ball as hard as he could. The ball sailed over everyone's head and broke the biggest window in the school. "From the first time I held a ball it sealed in the palm of my hand as though it belonged there," he later said, "and when I threw it, ball, hand and wrist, arm and shoulder and back seemed to all work together."

In 1902 the Johnson family moved to Olinda, a small town southeast of Los Angeles, so his father could take a job in the southern California oil fields. Walter became a regular at the local sandlots and soon gained a reputation as a strikeout king. Joe Burke, a bookkeeper for the semipro Santa Fe Railroad team and player-manager of the Olinda Oil Wells, heard the stories about him. One day Burke and Jack Burnet, a slugger for his team, decided to go down "and have some fun with the lads." He asked young Walt to throw him a few pitches. Johnson struck both men out with ease. He was then given a tougher tryout in a real game. On July 24, 1904, Olinda had a commanding lead over another semipro team from Los Angeles, and Burke decided to put Johnson and some other "youngsters" into the game. "Walt turned things loose," Burke would later recall, "and hanged if he didn't drub that Los Angeles bunch worse than we did." The final score was 21–6, and a local paper reported that "Johnson, the crack pitcher of the Olinda 'kid' team, fanned six men in the three innings which he worked."

Called "The Big Swede" because of his sandy brown hair, broad frame and sleepy eyes, Johnson actually traced his ancestry from the British Isles. He had what his grandson later described as "a short 'windmill' windup in which he rotated his arm in a circle while standing straight up on the mound, then swept the arm behind his back as far as it would go before whipping it forward in a smooth sidearm-underarm arc."

It didn't take long for word of Johnson's ability to get about, and soon major league scouts were coming to Olinda. Burke wasn't bothered. "I felt sure that if he had half a chance he would develop into something really great," he recalled later. "He was our kind of fellow. . . . We gave the lad the best support we had in us."

Johnson joined a minor league team in Tacoma, Washington. There a manager told Johnson he would make a better outfielder than pitcher, and released him. (The manager, Mike Lynch, would always be known as "The Man Who Let Walter Johnson Slip Away.") From Tacoma, Johnson went to Weiser, Idaho, a town of gold and copper miners, farmers, ranchers and cowboys—"a big-hearted, hard-fisted town," he would recall.

Before long Johnson, "The Weiser Wonder," was coming to the attention of the big leagues. In 1907 Rube Ellis, an outfielder for the Los Angeles Angels of the Pacific Coast League, spoke with awe to his manager, Frank "Pop" Dillon, about the young phenomenon he had faced in an off-season game. The Angels were a farm team for the Chicago Cubs and Dillon arranged to have Johnson meet him and Angels owner Hen Berry at the Hoffman, a cigar store and billiard parlor in Los Angeles. The episode would provide a comic example of two of Johnson's most outstanding traits: his humility and his diffidence. Johnson later described what happened:

> I was on time for the appointment and sat near the door where they would enter. They came in a little while after I arrived and immediately started playing a game of billiards. They didn't ask for me and didn't seem to be much concerned whether I had come or not. I didn't feel as though I ought to go up and interrupt such important men. Pretty soon their billiard game was finished and they left without knowing I was present.

Los Angeles' loss turned into Washington's gain. In 1907 the Senators' manager was Joe Cantillon, a funny but irascible man who had formerly been an umpire. "Pongo Joe" had been Clark Griffith's vaudeville partner in San Francisco's Barbary Coast; he loved cigars, wore a bright red vest, and was as outspoken as his future star was reticent. At a game he was umpiring, a player—some say it was John McGraw—kept complaining about the calls. In those days the umpire stood behind the pitcher, and when McGraw got a hit Cantillon whispered to the pitcher, who happened to be a player called Clark Griffith, to go ahead and pick him off first base. After an obvious balk, Griffith picked him off. McGraw howled with outrage, but Cantillon ignored him. When the next batter got on base, Griffith tried the same thing, but this time Cantillon called the balk. The first call, he explained to Griffith, had been "a personal favor."

Cantillon was known for his bluntness and sarcasm. Once when he was manager and the Senators played Detroit, his third baseman twice overthrew bunts by Ty Cobb, allowing Cobb to move to third base. The next time Cobb came up, Cantillon told the man to take the ball and, if it was a bunt, wait at third.

In the first two months of the 1907 season, the Senators struggled near the bottom of the standings. The team had no money for scouts, so Cantillon began sending players out to hunt for new talent. One of the players was catcher Cliff Blankenship, who was out of the lineup with a broken finger. In June, Blankenship was sent out west to take a look at an outfielder, Clyde Milan, and a young pitcher, Walter Johnson. Cantillon's friend, Joe "Mickey" Shea, had seen Johnson in California and had been sending Cantillon breathless notes about him for a year. "This boy throws so fast you can't see 'em," read one, "and he knows where he is throwing the ball because if he didn't there would be dead bodies strewn all over Idaho." The numbers for Johnson's 1907 Idaho season were staggering: 75 straight shutout innings, 166 strikeouts in 11 games. But on his scouting trip Blankenship was apparently kept in the dark about Johnson. He complained about having to go all the way to Idaho to see "some big busher that isn't even worth the car fare to scout."

Blankenship quickly changed his mind when he saw Johnson pitch. He offered him a contract to pitch for Washington, and was stunned when Johnson said no.

"Aren't you glad to get a chance in the East?" he asked.

"I've been East," was the innocent reply. "I was born in Kansas."

Johnson said he wasn't sure that he was ready for the majors. "I was nothing but a green country boy," he later said, "and jumping to a city the size of Washington was a real sensation to me." He doubted that his parents would approve. When they advised him to take the opportunity, Johnson agreed—but only after demanding that Blankenship give him enough train fare to return home if things didn't work out. Blankenship wired

Washington for $250 in expenses and handed Johnson $100. "I never did find out who got the change," Johnson later said.

On Friday, July 26, 1907, Walter Johnson arrived in Washington. He took a streetcar down Pennsylvania Avenue, getting off at Fifteenth Street by the Regent Hotel, close to the White House. It was a hot summer night, and there were three men sitting on the porch—Joe Cantillon and two umpires.

"Is this the hotel where the Washington ballplayers stop?" Johnson asked.

"Only the good ones," Cantillon replied sourly, not knowing who the young man was.

"Then I guess this is no place for me," the tall stranger said. He picked up his suitcase and started to leave when Cantillon asked him who he was.

"My name is Walter Johnson."

Billy Evans, one of the umpires there, said that Cantillon, who had been waiting for Johnson's train for two days, "jumped to his feet and greeted the youngster like a long lost brother."

The next day Johnson donned a Washington uniform to pitch batting practice to the Senators and the visiting White Sox. Cantillon told Johnson to take it easy, not to use too much speed. As one witness, umpire Bill Evans, put it, "The first ball Johnson sent up in practice looked like a small pea, and the more he pitched the smaller it seemed to get." Players were missing the ball—this in batting practice—and began talking among themselves.

Probably the best account came from Jim Delahanty (Ed's brother, and one of five Delahanty brothers to play baseball), the Senators' second baseman and the best hitter on the team:

> I never had time to take the bat off my shoulder. The ball shot right by me, right in the groove and was in the catcher's glove before I knew it had left the rookie's hand. And when he came back with another one in the same spot, I laid my bat down and walked over to manager Joe Cantillon, and said, "I'm through."
>
> "What's he got?" asked Joe. "Has he got a fast one?"
>
> "Fast one?" I replied. "No human ever threw a ball so fast before."
>
> "Has he got a curve?" Joe queried.

"I don't know and I don't care," I said. "What's more, I am not going back to find out until I know how good his control is."

Delahanty asked Cantillon when he planned to start the youngster. When Johnson looked ready, the manager replied. Delahanty said, "If ever there was a pitcher in baseball that was ready, that rube out there is the guy."

On August 7, 1907, Walter Johnson made his major debut against Ty Cobb and the Detroit Tigers. Eleven thousand standing-room-only Washington fans found it hard to believe that this tanned, lanky kid with the strange delivery was the messiah they had heard about. Johnson's grandson Henry Thomas has speculated that this was probably due to Johnson's slow windmill windup, which made it appear that he wasn't throwing very hard.

Before the game, Ty Cobb and the other Tigers heard that the Senators were starting a rookie—from Idaho, no less. They began making mooing sounds at Johnson and hectoring Joe Cantillon, telling him he was going to need to send this hayseed "back to the barn."

The Tigers' first batter was Davy Jones. Johnson wound up and fired a strike. "It was the fastest pitch I ever saw," Jones said later. He described Johnson as having arms "like whips."

Johnson got out the next two batters. At the top of the second inning, he faced Ty Cobb, who bunted and made it to first safely when Johnson bobbled the ball, then moved up to third when the next batter bunted. The next man singled to left, scoring Cobb.

Detroit won the game, 3–2, largely owing to errors by the Senators and aggressive baserunning—including an inside-the-park home run by Cobb. (In 1907 Cobb would emerge as a star, leading his team to a pennant. They would lose in the World Series to the Chicago Cubs.)

Although they were opposites, Johnson and Cobb became good friends. Where Johnson was taciturn and modest, and had come from a stable and close family, Cobb was violent, aggrieved, ruthless. When he was eighteen, his father, suspecting that Cobb's mother was cheating on him, tried to spy on her through the bedroom window. Cobb's mother was startled and mistakenly shot him. Writer Al Stump said that Cobb's desire to vindicate Cobb Sr. was the engine driving the "most violent, successful, thoroughly maladjusted personality ever to pass across American sports."

Like most of those who played against him, my grandfather couldn't stand the way Cobb slid into bases with his sharpened spikes high, the better to wound the fielder. My father once told me a story about it that, while not in any Cobb biography I researched, has been verified by other family members. One day before a game against Washington, Cobb waltzed over to the Senators' dugout and began filing his spikes in front of the club. My grandfather, or so the story goes, picked up a bat and climbed out of the dugout. He told Cobb that if he wanted to go to the hospital, just go right on doing what he was doing. Cobb backed down.

Cobb was disliked even by his own teammates: he had dined and traveled to the park alone since arriving in Detroit in 1905. But they were in awe of his ability. Indeed, upon his retirement Cobb's statistics would be unparalleled: a lifetime batting average of .367, over 4,000 hits, played in more games than any other player and stole more bases.

It would be hard to imagine a man more ill-suited to be friends with Walter Johnson, but they genuinely liked each other. "In eighteen years, I have never had an unfriendly word with Cobb," Johnson once said. "I consider him to be one of my friends." Cobb concurred: "We were friends at all times—on the diamond or across a poker table." Cobb once took Johnson for a ride in a new car, a trip that resulted in a speeding citation. Cobb bribed his way out by offering the policeman two tickets to that day's game. The cop responded that Cobb could pay for the citation by hitting two home runs, which he did.

Walter Johnson's first game serves as an epitome of most of the Senators' games until the mid-1920s. For years Johnson was surrounded by some of the most inept players in baseball, yet he managed to win games, or keep them close, and break records. In 21 seasons with the Senators (10 with second division teams),

Johnson would win 417 games, second only to Cy Young. He pitched 110 shutouts, 38 by the score of 1–0, which is still a record.

Pitchers during Johnson's era were not restricted by pitch counts or five days' rest between starts, and Johnson's stamina had to be phenomenal. In 1908, he shut out the New York Yankees three times in four days. His first game was a six-hitter and a 3–0 victory. The next day he pitched a four-hitter, giving Washington a 6–0 victory. After a day off—there was no Sunday baseball in New York at the time—Johnson was forced to pitch when two Washington players were benched due to injury and a cold. He tossed a two-hitter, and the New York crowd gave him a standing ovation. The *New York Times* commented archly:

> We are grievously disappointed in this man Johnson of Washington. He and his team had four games to play with the champion Yankees. Johnson pitched the first game and shut us out. Johnson pitched the second game and shut us out. Johnson pitched the third game and shut us out. Did Johnson pitch the fourth game and shut us out? He did not. Oh, you quitter!

Johnson's power was such that, at least in the early days, there was apparently only one man who could catch him, Charles "Gabby" Street, who got his nickname from his constant talk during games. "Gabby was always jabbering," Johnson once said, "and he never let a pitcher take his mind off the game." Street had a powerful arm, and when there was a man on first he would exclaim, "Let 'em run, Gabby'll get 'em!"

Street was the only man who could handle Johnson's heat, but in July 1910, as the Senators were limping through another dismal season, Street got hurt. The Senators had two backup catchers, but neither of them could cope with Johnson. The first catcher was, as the *Washington Post* reported, "put out of commission after about six pitched balls." The second, added the *Post,* "would never have lasted the game had Johnson not stopped hurling smoke balls over." Years later umpire Billy Evans would call a game because of darkness when an inexperienced catcher mishandled a Johnson pitch and it grazed Evans's ear. Evans quipped that a couple more innings weren't worth dying for.

At the end of the 1908 season the Senators had a chance to avoid the bottom of the standings for the first time. The Philadelphia Athletics arrived in Washington on September 11 for a five-game series, and if Washington could win a game they would end the season in seventh rather than eighth place. During the opening game, Johnson faced a young player named "Shoeless" Joe Jackson, playing in his second major league game. Jackson, who would become infamous in the 1919 "Black Sox" scandal when his teammates threw the World Series, got one of the nine hits the Athletics managed off Johnson. The Senators won 2–1.

Johnson called Jackson "the greatest natural hitter I ever saw." He also felt that Washington hadn't deserved to win against Philadelphia because the Senators hadn't played very well. Ed Grillo, a reporter for the *Washington Post,* was impressed by this admission. He wrote of Johnson:

> There is something about this boy aside from his ability as a pitcher, that makes him popular with patrons of the game. He is absolutely honest in everything he does. He never complains of the umpires' decisions and is modest to a fault, believing that his teammates, more than himself, are entitled to the credit for what his team accomplishes when he is playing.

Years later Grillo would witness another display of Johnson's embarrassment at winning ugly. In a close game, the Senators let three men on base due to errors, and Johnson had to strike out the next three. Heading back to the dugout, he kept his head down. "Look at him!" Senators manager Cantillon exclaimed. "He's ashamed he did it!" It was no surprise when Johnson was voted the most popular player in the *Washington Post* poll of 1908.

Walter Johnson was virtually a one-man team, but he couldn't win games entirely on his own. The 1909 season would be even worse for him—indeed, the worst season the Senators would ever have. The team still holds two records from that year: the fewest runs scored in a season, 380, and the most times shut out in one season, 24. Johnson went 13–25. The pennant was taken by Detroit, led by Ty Cobb, who hit .377 and led the American League in homers and RBIs.

But there was hope for better days. The arrival of a new manager, Clark Griffith, a man who would bring Washington to unprecedented baseball glory, was right around the corner. And a young Irishman named Joe Judge was turning heads playing first base on the sandlots of New York.

GRIFFITH'S MEN

My grandfather was born in 1894, a year before Babe Ruth. He batted and threw left-handed, and he was small for a first baseman at 5'7" and 150 pounds. Described as "a wrist hitter," he used a bat weighing 37 ounces. He choked up about four inches, "and when he swings he gets a quick swap of his wrist behind the blow." This was the stance of a slap hitter, someone who could drive out singles, doubles and triples but not home runs—especially not in cavernous American League Park. In fact, he hit only 71 homers in his career. In style, he was the anti-Ruth.

The idea that his son could make money by playing a game must have seemed incredible to my great-grandfather, Joseph Patrick Judge, a poor Irish farmer from County Mayo who immigrated to New York in 1883. J. P. Judge became a U.S. citizen on October 17, 1888, and three years later married Catherine Hanley. Joseph got a job working for the Edison Electric Company, and the couple settled into a tough Irish neighborhood in Brooklyn. On May 30, 1894, Catherine gave birth to my grandfather.

Joe Judge was left-handed, which was considered a moral as well as a physical problem in parenting manuals of the day. Teachers could not break his "habit" of using his left hand for writing or swinging a bat. He played on the "midget teams" until he went to school at St. Vincent Ferrer School. At twelve he was the star of the Delmar Club, a team that won, according to one paper, "the championship of Central Park." Granddad, like a lot of immigrants' kids at the time, lived in a sink-or-swim world. In fact, his mother taught him to swim by tying a rope around his waist and dropping him in the East River. (Although I assume she did this in shallow water near the shore, my mental picture of this is always of a small boy struggling in rough, stormy waters.) In spite—or because—of this perfunctory method of instruction, Joe became a good swimmer. When he was a boy, he and two friends swam out to Riker's Island, but the guards at the prison wouldn't let them land, holding them off with guns, so they had to turn around and return home. One of his friends didn't make it and drowned.

Dropping out of school after eighth grade, in 1911 Joe began playing ball for his father's company team, the Edison Nine. By 1913 he had moved up to Brooklyn's Dexter Park semipro team. That same year he was scouted by Giants manager John McGraw, who told him that he was too small for a first baseman and suggested that he become a pitcher. This irritated my grandfather, and years later he was glad finally to get revenge against the Giants' Little Napoleon.

It was around this time that the Judge family—my grandfather had a brother and two sisters—moved to Yorkville, a cramped Lower East Side neighborhood of Jews, Italians, Hungarians and Irish. No one in my family remembers exactly where the house was, but my grandfather left an important clue as to the milieu: his neighbor was a kid named Jimmy Cagney. Cagney once recalled Yorkville this way: "It always sticks in my memory as [a place] of stark tragedy. There was always a crepe hanging on a door or two. Somewhere on the block there was always the clanging of an ambulance bell. Padock wagons came often." To both Joe Judges it might not have seemed like much of an improvement over the deprivation of Ireland.

After his father moved the family to Yorkville, Joe joined the semipro Yorkville Orients. It was while he was in Yorkville that Judge met a man who changed his life.

Bud Hannah, a neighborhood mailman, always stopped by the field during his daily round to watch the players practice.

One afternoon he noticed the small, skinny kid the other players called "Josie" playing shortstop. My grandfather recounted
years later:

> [Hannah] told me I was wasting my time playing short, that
> a left-hander could never play that position in the big leagues.
> And I had my heart set on making it to the big leagues even
> then. He told me to get a first baseman's mitt and start prac-
> ticing with it as soon as possible. Well, I was a poor kid and
> I told him the finger glove was all I was likely to own in the
> way of baseball equipment in the years to come.

Hannah appeared at the field the next day. He called Judge over
and handed him a box. According to my grandfather,

> [I]nside was the most beautiful first baseman's mitt I've ever
> seen, before or since. I don't know how he could afford it.
> Mailmen didn't get much in those days. It must have set him
> back a week's pay.

For the rest of his career, whenever the Senators were in
New York to play the Yankees, Joe Judge left a pair of tickets at
the gate for Hannah and went over to speak to him—a clear violation of rules put into place after the 1919 Black Sox scandal,
when Commissioner Kenesaw Mountain Landis forbade players
from fraternizing with fans in an effort to eliminate opportuni-
ties for gambling. At first, Joe's sense of obligation to his benefac-
tor outweighed Landis's injunction. "It was little enough for me
to do for him after all he had done for me," he said. As a result,
he started getting hit with fines. "I picked up the paper one day
in 1921," he once told an interviewer, "and read that I had been
fined $50 for talking to someone in the stands. If you played ball
for Washington in those days, $50 was a princely sum."

So the next time the Senators were in New York to play the
Yankees, Joe left the tickets for Hannah as usual but didn't go
over to talk to him. "Gee, I was embarrassed," he recalled. "Hannah kept calling to me, and I guess he had been bragging to his
pal that he knew me. But I was afraid to go near him. I thought
Commissioner Landis might suspend me." The next day my

grandfather left tickets, but Hannah failed to show. And when Hannah failed to show for the rest of the series, Grandpa began feeling terrible, and his play reflected it. "I had been hitting around .325 all season," he said, "and then my average fell down around .260. I couldn't seem to buy an extra base hit."

A few weeks later, Judge was still in a slump when the Senators returned to New York. At the opening game, Hannah's regular seat was empty. Grandpa went to Senators owner Clark Griffith and explained the situation. Griffith said, "Joe, my boy, you get that man, Hannah, out to this ball park tomorrow if you have to drag him. Then go over and talk to him all you want. Have your picture taken if you want. I'll worry about Landis."

Joe called on Hannah at his house and brought him to the park, explaining what had happened on the way. At the park he talked to Hannah and his boss, had pictures taken and gave them both an autographed ball.

The following day Landis leveled a $100 fine, which Griffith promptly paid. The next game, Judge talked to Hannah again, incurring another fine, which Griffith also paid. This went on for a year, then abruptly stopped. "I guess Landis just got tired of the whole thing," my grandfather said. After resuming his friendship with the old postman, his average quickly went up and he ended the 1921 season once again hitting over .300.

$\mathcal{O}$

BY 1914 JOE WAS PLAYING in the New England League for the Buffalo Bisons, a farm team for the Boston Red Sox. It was here that he was discovered, first by his wife and then by the Washington Senators. He was in Kenosha, Vermont, for a game when, while crossing the street, he was seen by 24-year-old Alma Gauvreau, a petite, pretty redhead from nearby Essex Junction, Vermont. Her father had run out on the family, leaving her mother to try and make ends meet by running a small store. The family was French Canadian, and Alma's first language was French.

My family has often marveled at how my grandmother and grandfather got together, given how different they were from each other. But it was that difference, of course, that provided the spark. While Joe Judge was shy, my grandmother was gregarious. He was largely abstemious (although he and a few players were known to cook up some bathtub gin at Judge's house during Prohibition), while Alma loved a drink and a smoke now and then. She referred to herself as "the second prettiest girl in Essex Junction"—she never said who was first—and early photos back up the claim. She was small and became even smaller in later years as I was growing up in the 1970s and 1980s; she couldn't have been more than five feet tall when she died in 1987.

My late father, who went into journalism instead of baseball, once wrote me a letter while he was traveling in Toronto for *National Geographic* in which he expressed pride in the French and Irish heritage of the family:

> It [strikes] me that you are descended from dissident minority peoples, the Irish who suffered under the English yoke for 800 years in County Mayo, God help us, and the French who were considered the blacks of Canada by overbearing English rulers. You come from illiterate peasant stock who were poor country farm folk, the losers in the political wars of their ancestors. And just as the Irish Judges were descended from the Brehons, people of learning and power, so in Canada the Gauvreaus were a powerful people in old French Canada.

Dad then traced the decline of both groups—largely at the hands of the British, or so he imagined—and noted how the Gauvreaus wound up in Vermont, "speaking French in an English-speaking country just as Joseph Patrick Judge was speaking Irish in English New York."

☾

WHILE THE TEENAGE JOE JUDGE was beginning his climb through the minors, the Senators were continuing to struggle. They finished next to last in 1908, with a record of 67–85. Walter Johnson went 14–14, pitching seven complete games.

Johnson got an $800 raise for 1909, bringing his salary to $3,500. But it would be his worst year. He caught a severe cold during spring training in Galveston, Texas, and didn't regain his full power for two months. His first game on April 24 resulted in a 17–0 pounding at the hands of New York. Although he had a disastrous 0–5 start, by June he had evened his record to 8–8. Around that time Joe Cantillon was offered $30,000 by the Yankees for Johnson and Gabby Street, but Cantillon replied that if he sold them he might as well unload the entire team. Cantillon was wise, because even a weakened Johnson was a formidable pitcher: in 1909 he was second in the league in strikeouts with 164 and innings with 296. He set a record for shutouts in a month—five in July. He went 13–25 with an ERA of 2.22, the only time in his first ten years as a major leaguer that his earned run average was above two runs.

Even though the team remained in the cellar, Washington was attracting some prominent fans. In 1909 President William Howard Taft attended a game. Apparently there was no advance word, because the *Washington Post* reported that "the game was interrupted by cheering [when Taft showed up], which spread . . . from the grandstand to the bleachers as the crowd recognized the president." Despite interest from the executive branch, however, the Senators finished 56 games behind Detroit.

The team had acquired a couple of new players who helped morale, Herman "Germany" Schaefer from Detroit and Nick Altrock, who had been a good pitcher for the White Sox before being released to a minor league Kansas City club. Altrock would win only one game for Washington, and Schaefer never developed into much of a player, but together they formed a comedy team that would become enormously popular in baseball. Starting in 1912, Altrock and Schaefer performed on the sidelines of games, usually selections from a repertoire of 150 pantomime routines. The two would work together for seven years, until Schaefer got a coaching job with John McGraw's Giants. After that his place was taken by Al Schacht, a pitcher who would play a significant part in the history of the Senators and of baseball itself.

Joe Cantillon was fired after the disastrous 1909 season, and Jimmy McAleer was hired to replace him. McAleer had previously managed the St. Louis Browns, finishing in the top four only three times in eight years. The Senators would remain awful under McAleer, finishing seventh in 1910 and 1911. McAleer's tenure began impressively, however. On April 4, 1910, President

Taft came to American Park to throw out the first pitch, the first time a president did so. McAleer had asked Walter Johnson to receive the toss, but the pitcher was too shy to accept the honor. The president wound up to deliver the ball to Gabby Street, but at the last second, despite his 300-pound bulk, Taft deftly shifted position and shot the ball to Johnson, who was standing nearby. The *Washington Post* reported that "President Taft, in spite of a big bay window, threw the ball with the finesse and grace of an accomplished player." That wasn't the only excitement in the presidential box: during the game Secretary of State Charles Bennett was beaned by a foul ball hit by the Philadelphia Athletics' Frank "Home Run" Baker. Aides began to swarm Bennett until he waved them off.

Despite their intractable hold on last place, the Senators got a brilliant season out of Walter Johnson. He led the majors in strikeouts, innings pitched and complete games, with an ERA of 1.35.

Washington would stay in the cellar for 1911, although Johnson would again have a great year, going 23–15. At the end of the season Jimmy McAleer announced that he was leaving the club, having bought a partnership in the Boston Red Sox. Then the Senators found their destiny when they selected Clark Griffith as their new manager.

Griffith's last year as player-manager of the White Sox had been in 1902, and from there he had gone to New York to pitch for and manage the Highlanders (soon to become the Yankees). In 1903, Griffith, age thirty-three, went 14–10 with an ERA of 2.70. The Highlanders almost took the pennant in 1906, but the team declined rapidly. In 1908 Griffith resigned, then managed the Cincinnati Reds for three years.

In 1911, after Jimmy McAleer left Washington, the Senators' owners approached Griffith about managing the hapless team. Shrewd in business as well as on the mound, Griffith agreed, with the proviso that he intended to be not only the manager but the largest shareholder in the Washington club. In the spring of 1911 Washington's American League Park burned down, and in order to build another park, the owners had to double the club's stock from $100,000 to $200,000. Griffith wanted in. After being turned down for a loan by his old friends Ban Johnson and Charles Comiskey (the latter telling Griffith that Washington was "a baseball graveyard"), Griffith sold his Montana farm for $20,000 and made his investment. On October 27, 1911, Griffith signed a contract with the Senators that called for him to be paid $7,500 a year.

The Old Fox's arrival in Washington catalyzed the team. Griffith immediately fired ten players and began to compile what he would call "my little ball club." The "Griffmen," as some newspaper writers began to call them, would not consist of home run hitters—especially considering the dimensions of the park that would soon be rechristened with Griffith's name. Instead, Griffith built around quick, defensive players who could get hits. Third baseman Eddie "Kid" Foster was a typical Griffith player. Foster wound up his career with the fewest home runs of any major league player with more than 5,000 at-bats, but he was such an outstanding contact hitter that Griffith created a new play for him, "the run and hit." If there was a player on base when Foster came up, he would run as soon as the pitcher delivered, confident that Foster would get his bat on the ball.

Griffith had team meetings every day at 9 A.M. He would end them by shouting, "What pitcher do we fear the most?" The team roared back: "There ain't none!" Griffith was fiercely loyal and compassionate, virtues he would display years later when he became full owner of the team. On one occasion he was chiding a reporter who had criticized the Senators, and when the writer defended himself by saying that 90 percent of what he had written was positive, Griffith shot back a conversation-stopping non sequitur: "You don't poison a man then claim you're doing him a favor when you pump his stomach!" Another time, Griffith picked up a newspaper and saw a picture of a widow and her small children who had been evicted from their home. He ordered an aide to bring the woman to see him. He rented a house for her and then set her up with a job in government by calling a friendly congressman.

Griffith's enthusiasm quickly turned a losing team into a winning one. After a dismal 1912 training camp in Charlottesville, Virginia—it snowed the entire time and the players spent all day shoveling—the Senators got off to a sluggish start, going 17–21 through the end of May. Griffith needed a good first baseman among other players, and borrowed $12,000 to pick up Charles "Chick" Gandil. Unlike my grandfather, Gandil actually looked like a first baseman: he was 6'2" and almost 200 pounds. Like most players back then, he had been toughened up by life. At seventeen he had run away from home in St. Paul, ending up playing baseball in Mexico. He also boxed, bringing in $150 a fight, and in the off season worked in a copper mine.

Gandil provided a spark for Washington, which didn't lose for three weeks, winning sixteen games, all of them on the road. When the team returned in June, President Taft threw out the first ball on June 18, having missed the official Opening Day because of the *Titanic* disaster, which had claimed one of his friends. The Senators downed the Athletics 5–4. They were in second place, where they would stay for most of the season. Johnson didn't lose for two months; his record would be 33–12 with a 1.39 ERA, the lowest in the league. Chick Gandil and center fielder Clyde Milan were brilliant—Milan had 88 stolen bases, outdistancing Ty Cobb's record by five. But the Senators faded and the Boston Red Sox won the pennant.

This was the year when Johnson acquired one of his nicknames, "Barney." Johnson bought his first car, and was driving around with Clyde Milan and Germany Schaefer when he was stopped for speeding. Schaefer told the officer that Johnson was "Barney Oldfield, the famous race car driver." The cop bought the story and let the men go, and that afternoon Johnson struck out nine batters with, as he said, "nothing but a fastball." When the tenth went down Schaefer called out, "Barney Oldfield's got nothing on him for speed!" (Johnson's more enduring nickname, "The Big Train," would be coined by a *Washington Post* writer in 1915.)

Washington came back strong in 1913, with Johnson having one of the greatest seasons in baseball history. He won 36 and lost 7, and led the league in strikeouts (243), shutouts (4), complete games (29), innings (346) and winning percentage (.837). He had winning streaks of 14, 10 and 7 games. "Barney" even batted .261, had a .423 slugging average and was without error in the field. The Senators ended the season in second place, with a record of 90–64. In the World Series, Connie Mack's Philadelphia Athletics defeated McGraw's Giants.

Johnson's 1913 ERA is listed in the books as 1.14, a record that stood until 1968, when Bob Gibson turned in a 1.12. But Johnson's ERA was actually 1.09. Why the discrepancy?

By October 4, the Senators had been mathematically eliminated from winning the pennant. On that day they faced the Red Sox in a game that was strictly for laughs. Johnson played center field, and neither team kept very strict official scoring. The Senators' right fielder, Germany Schaefer, spent most of the game in the infield or sitting on a Bull Durham sign in the outfield. At times Al Schacht lay down on the field and pretended to be sleeping. At the end of eight innings, the Senators were up 10–3 when a group of about a thousand soldiers who had come to the game demanded to see Johnson pitch. Catching Johnson was Jack Ryan, a 43-year-old coach who hadn't played in a major league game since 1903. Johnson gingerly tossed a couple of fat pitches over the plate, giving up two hits before heading back to the outfield. The two token hits would raise his ERA and allow Gibson to break the record.

Despite the improvements, the Senators couldn't break into first place. Griffith knew he needed more offense, and while the team was in Detroit he presented Tigers owner Frank Navin a check for $100,000 for the premier hitter in baseball, Ty Cobb. Griffith didn't have the money to cover the check, but as usual he had a scheme. He would sell $100,000 worth of advance tickets, telling Washington fans that the money was going toward Cobb's purchase. "You'll have to give me time to work on that check," he told Navin, "but I'll make it good if it buys Cobb. Give me two weeks." Navin agreed to think about it.

When the news of Griffith's maneuvering got back to Washington, the Senators' board of directors told Griffith he was insane, and immediately turned down the deal.

Ω

AFTER THE SENATORS FINISHED THIRD in 1914, Griffith again went out looking for talent. In early 1915, he traveled to Buffalo to scout a promising center fielder, Charles "Kid" Jameson. Griffith was prepared to offer the minor league Buffalo team $7,000 for him, but when he saw the team in play, it was another player—a young man named Joe Judge—who caught his eye. Judge had gone four for four in the league championship game against Providence, and his fielding statistics were impressive. Griffith told the Buffalo owners that he wanted Jameson, "but that young first baseman Judge ought to be thrown in on the deal." The owners balked at giving away a player and insisted on getting something in return. Griffith wound up paying an extra $500 for him.

On September 20, 1915, the game in Washington started ten minutes late. The next day, the papers reported the reason why: a new young player, Joe Judge, had been on his way down from New England, but his train was late. Judge was in the locker room at starting time, changing as fast as he could.

Joe liked to talk about the moment he first emerged from the dugout and saw the ball park. "It just was so huge," he used to say. He got a couple of hits in his first game. "Griffith is very much impressed with Judge's ability as a hitter and a speed artist," reported the *Washington Star*. Griffith enthused about the way Judge waited for the right pitch and, as a left-hander, could hit left-handed pitchers. At this point Griffith traded Chick Gandil, who would ultimately make his way to Chicago and gain infamy during the 1919 Black Sox scandal.

Because he arrived on the squad so late in the season, Joe got to play in only twelve games in 1915. He made 17 hits for a .375 average and the team finished fourth. That year the World Series was won by the Boston Red Sox, who had just signed an impressive new young pitcher named George Herman Ruth, whom everyone called "Babe." Both Philadelphia manager Connie Mack and John McGraw had passed on him.

Ruth had grown up on the streets of Baltimore, and like McGraw, Cobb and other baseball players, in very difficult circumstances. His mother died when he was seventeen; his saloonkeeper father remarried and then was killed in a street fight with his new brother-in-law. At age seven Ruth had been placed in St. Mary's Industrial Home for Boys, run by the Brothers of the

Xaverian Order for wayward and criminal kids. Writers have often suggested that Ruth's grim childhood led to his giant appetites—for women, drink and food—that couldn't possibly be satisfied. "Ruth's mean, untutored youth ill-fitted him for the sudden fortune and fame that fell to him," thinks the noted baseball historian Harold Seymour. "No doubt it accounts for much of his unrestrained pursuit of hedonistic pleasures."

Yet around the time Boston was acquiring Ruth, Washington brought on a player whose life challenges that theory. In 1915, along with Joe Judge, Griffith signed an outfielder named Edgar "Sam" Rice, who was then twenty-five, old for a rookie. It was not for nearly eighty years, until a 1993 article in *Sports Illustrated,* that anyone knew why Rice got such a late start in the big leagues.

He was born in 1890 and raised on a farm in Morocco, Indiana. In 1908 he married Beulah Stam, and they moved to Watseka, Illinois. The couple had two children and Rice worked a variety of different jobs, but he was desperate to play baseball. In April 1912, at age twenty-two, he was at last asked to try out for a minor league team in Galesburg, Illinois. While he was gone, Beulah took the kids to Rice's parents. Along with Rice's two younger sisters, the family went to the nearby town of Iroquois to visit friends.

Returning at around 6 P.M., the family looked up at the darkening skies where racks of clouds were moving in swiftly from the southwest—a dire warning sign. They rushed inside to take refuge, but at 6:30 their house took a direct hit from the tornado. A local newspaper described the aftermath:

> Its work there was almost too terrible to relate. The house was blown entirely away as were the other buildings but for a tool shed which was untouched. The timbers of the house and barn were scattered for nearly a quarter of a mile to the southeast. The furniture and contents of the house were twisted into shapes which would seem impossible to accomplish, and when the wreck had passed every member of the family except Mr. Rice [Sr.] lay dead either in the yard or adjoining fields. . . . The bodies were found as far as 60 rods from the house, nearly stripped of clothes, bruised and broken.

Sam Rice stayed by his father's side for a week, but Charles Rice was devastated by the tragedy and died shortly after. For decades, Sam Rice would not speak of the catastrophe, not even to the woman he later married at the age of thirty-nine. She only discovered the truth when Rice was being interviewed by a reporter in the mid-1960s.

After his loss, Rice worked odd jobs and drifted for a year before joining the Navy. A crewman aboard the USS *New Hampshire,* he became her star pitcher. The ship was berthed at Portsmouth, Virginia, and he was able to pitch for the Virginia League during furloughs. Clark Griffith had loaned money to the Petersburg Club of the Virginia League, and when it folded he accepted Rice as payment for the debt.

Late in life, Griffith called Sam Rice "the best all-around ballplayer we ever had." He would average a lifetime .322 as the Senators' all-time best hitter. He had more than 200 hits in six seasons and fell just 13 hits shy of 3,000 for his career. Overcoming a tragedy that dwarfed Ruth's, Sam Rice was a solid citizen through and through.

Sam Rice and Joe Judge were teammates for eighteen seasons, which was a record for six decades. They were also friends who bought row houses next to each other, at 711 (Judge) and 713 (Rice) Allison Street in Petworth, a neighborhood just a short trolley ride up a hill from the ball park. Joe's daughters, my aunts Anita and Dorothy, remember the Rice household as a very strict environment. Dorothy remembered them as nice people who insisted on good manners. "When you were at their house," she said, "you had to sit straight up with your hands folded. You couldn't fidget around."

IN THE SECOND DECADE OF the new century, baseball players were beginning to earn real money for a game that only recently had been considered a diversion for amateurs. The sport's *nouveaux riches* caused tut-tutting among some sportswriters, as in a 1914 editorial in *Baseball* magazine:

It is, as a rule, a man's business how he spends his money. But nevertheless we wish to call attention to the fact that many men do so in an unwise manner. A very glaring instance of this among baseball players is the recent evil tendency to purchase and maintain automobiles. Put the money away, boys, where it will be safe. You don't need those automobiles. The money will look mighty good later on in life. Think it over, boys.

In fact, most ball players couldn't afford a new car. Although there were stars like Walter Johnson, the era of the superstar home run blaster who would become a national celebrity was still ten years off.

Most players in the 1910s who led the major leagues in home runs hit an average of ten. The high for the decade was 316 in 1911, scored by the National League; the greatest hitter was Ty Cobb, who hit .387, with nine batting titles, 160 triples, eight slugging averages over .500, but only 48 home runs. Before his disgrace, Joe Jackson hit .354 for the decade and led the league in triples twice, in 1912 and 1916.

Change began when a new, livelier ball was introduced in 1911. The cork-centered ball had been used in the 1910 World Series, and when it entered major league play in 1911 there was a burst of new offense. Pitchers' earned run averages went from 3.02 to 3.39 in the National League and from 2.53 to 3.34 in the American League. Cobb and Jackson both hit over .400 in 1911. But the pitchers seemed to get used to the new ball; ERAs dropped again in 1913.

The early 1900s had been dominated by pitching, with legendary hurlers Christy Mathewson, Cy Young and Mordecai "Three Fingers" Brown dominating the sport. The 1910s continued the trend with Walter Johnson, who had a 1.59 ERA for the decade and averaged a 29–13 record, and a brilliant young pitcher named Babe Ruth, who went 89–46 from 1914 to 1919, including three wins in two World Series for Boston.

The 1910s also saw the construction of new ball parks all over the country. Between 1909, when Philadelphia's Shibe Park went up, and 1923, when Yankee Stadium was built, fourteen teams acquired new parks. They were made of concrete and steel, a change from the wood structures of the past. Comiskey Park in Chicago, Fenway Park in Boston, Tigers Stadium in Detroit and Wrigley Field in Chicago were cathedrals to the new sports religion of baseball, which attracted a worshipful public.

Washington shared in the excitement, although after two second-place finishes in 1912 and 1913, the Senators began to struggle. The team finished third in 1914, fourth in Joe Judge's first season in 1915, and back down to seventh in 1916, despite Walter Johnson's 25–20 record. The Big Train lost out to Babe Ruth for ERA leader of the American League.

Babe Ruth made up one-half of a rare two-man no-hitter in major league history. On June 23, 1917, the Senators were in Boston. In the first inning Ruth was pitching to the Senators' lead-off hitter, Ray Morgan, when umpire Brick Owen called four close balls, sending Ruth into a rage. He stormed the plate to complain, and when Owen kicked him out of the game Ruth took a swing at the umpire and had to be forcibly removed from the field. He was replaced by Ernie Shore. Ray Morgan on first was thrown out trying to steal second, then Shore went on to throw nine no-hit innings. American League president Ban Johnson agreed to score it a no-hitter for Shore.

That same year, Griffith temporarily lost one of his best players when Joe Judge broke his leg while sliding into second base against Detroit. Griffith had promised Judge a $500 bonus if he hit .285 or better (he had hit a disappointing .220 in 1916). He was hitting .273 when the Senators played the Yankees in Washington on August 13. He went 8 for 14 against New York and then went 2 for 4 in the first game against Detroit, raising his average to .286. He failed to get a hit his first two times at bat in the second game. The third time up he got a base on balls, dropping his average to .285. It was then that he broke his leg. He was $500 richer and out for the rest of the season.

During his rehabilitation, Judge discovered something he would always say was key to his longevity: the importance of strong legs. He claimed that he often saw veteran players having to quit when their legs "went back on them." For several weeks prior to every spring training, he would go to the gym and do exercises to build up his leg muscles. He devoted what was then considered an inordinate amount of time to loosening up his leg muscles before a game.

Strong legs couldn't keep him or any other player out of the draft, however; it would take a special deferment. On July 19, 1918, Secretary of War Newton D. Baker announced that baseball players would have to serve in the war. Earlier in the year he had issued a "work or fight" order announcing that all able-bodied men of draft age had to either enlist or do work that was considered essential to the war effort. There had been some hope that Baker would exempt baseball. After the July order, however, the Senators lost several players, including their catcher Eddie Ainsmith (who had taken over from Gabby Street) and Sam Rice. Joe Judge, married and with a new baby daughter— my aunt Catherine—got a deferment.

Despite the shortened season, the Senators didn't let up on their workhorse. Walter Johnson pitched 325 innings in 1918, just three fewer than he had the previous season. He went 23–13 and led the majors in strikeouts with 162. He finished every game he played in, 29 starts and 10 relief jobs. He even hit .267. The team finished in third place, only four games behind Babe Ruth's Red Sox, who would win the World Series over the Cubs.

In 1919, the Senators finished seventh, their worst position in ten years. Yet even as the White Sox were throwing the Series that year, Griffith was adding to his offensive foundation of Walter Johnson, Joe Judge and Sam Rice in right field; he signed Tom Zachary, a tall, quiet 23-year-old tobacco farmer from North Carolina who would win fifteen or more games a season as a pitcher in four of the next five years, including a crucial victory in the 1924 World Series.

Another Griffith acquisition in 1919 would turn out to be one of his best. The player was first noticed by scout Joe Engel. Griffith had met Engel in 1912, at Engel's Beer Garden on E Street in Washington. The place was owned by Engel's German father and frequented by writers of the *Washington Post,* whose offices were across the street. Engel's father introduced his boy Joe, who at eighteen was 6'2" and almost 200 pounds. Griffith tried Engel out as a pitcher, but he never really got control of his fastball, so Griffith agreed to hire him as a scout.

Engel was affable and gregarious, a sharp judge of talent and a canny negotiator. He reasoned that "a fellow will do more for a friend than a stranger," so he softened up his potential recruits and their managers by bringing their children presents. In choosing a player, Engel went on instinct rather than hard statistics; he was interested in "how a player handles himself" as much as numbers on a page.

In the fall of 1919, Griffith sent Engel on his first assignment to Binghamton, New York, to look at a pitcher named Pat Martin. Binghamton was playing Buffalo, but Engel wasn't very impressed with Martin. Instead, he focused on the Buffalo second baseman. Early in the game a fight broke out, and Engel was amazed that the second baseman had taken on a player twice his size. Engel called Griffith and told him about the tough infielder, whose name was Stanley Harris. Griffith already knew about him; Joe Judge had played with Harris on a Baltimore shipyard team the year before and recommended him, but Griffith wasn't convinced that Harris was much of a hitter. Engel was insistent, however, so Griffith got on a train for Binghamton to see for himself.

The two men watched Harris get six hits and a walk in his eight trips to the plate during a doubleheader. But Griffith still wasn't won over. After the game he went to the locker room to meet Harris. He found the second baseman unwrapping tape from his fingers and realized that Harris had played despite a broken finger. It was a typical act of toughness. Harris had been reared in the coalfields of Pittston, Pennsylvania. His grandfather was a "fire boss," the man who made 2 A.M. safety inspections to determine if the miners could go down into the shafts. At the age of twelve Harris was working as a breaker boy, responsible for separating slate from coal into buckets as it came down. The job gave him his nickname: Bucky.

Griffith signed him on the spot.

$\mathcal{O}$

DESPITE GRIFFITH'S GOOD EYE FOR players, however, Washington was still struggling, mostly against the New York Yankees.

In the 1919 off season New York had made what would become the most brilliant acquisition in baseball history, buying Babe Ruth from the cash-poor Red Sox. His arrival heralded the decade of the great Yankee dynasties, which were built largely at the expense of other teams, especially the Red Sox; their owner, Harry Frazee, was always investing in Broadway shows, and to pay for those extravaganzas he was often forced to sell his best players. In 1920 Frazee sold Ruth for $125,000 and a $300,000 loan.

While the New York teams were building dynasties, Clark Griffith was putting together a sharp team of his own. He knew that if he wanted a championship he would have to assemble a team before Walter Johnson passed his prime. By 1920, Griffith's last year as manager before becoming the team's owner, the Senators ended the year in sixth place, and Johnson began showing signs of slowing down—or at least of being human. Johnson was thirty-two, which was then considered old for a major league player. He had come down with another bad cold after thirteen straight nights on a Pullman train, and at one point had trouble lifting his arm over his head. He struggled all season. Ironically, it was also the year he would throw the only no-hitter of his career.

It happened on July 1. The Senators were in Boston to play the Red Sox. The game came down to a duel between Johnson and Boston's Harry Hooper. Washington was ahead 1–0 and Johnson had a no-hitter going when outfielder Harry Harper came up in the bottom of the ninth inning. On the second pitch from Johnson, Harper, a lefty, pulled the ball sharply towards right field. As one writer described it, the ball "streaked bullet-like and struck the ground a few feet in front of first base. It went over the bag on a sizzling bounce and appeared to be on its way to give Harper an extra-base hit and kill Johnson's bid for a no hitter."

But Joe Judge was playing deep and had broken left as soon as the ball left Harper's bat. He threw himself to the ground in shallow right field while snagging the ball, quickly tossing to Johnson covering at first. Harper was out by half a step. Judge went into a happy "war dance" as Johnson jumped on his back. "I never knew how heavy he was until then," Granddad once recalled. "I was only 150 pounds and I was carrying much more than that." Even the Boston fans cheered—in fact, Harry Hooper was the first one to congratulate Johnson.

The game had taken a lot out of Johnson. The next day he was scheduled to pitch the second game of a doubleheader against the Yankees, but pulled a muscle in his leg while warming up. He also told Griffith that his arm hurt. Griffith went into a panic—a record crowd of eighteen thousand had come to see a Senators victory. Griffith turned to the pitching staff, telling them that he was in "a desperate spot" and that one of them had to fill in for the Big Train. There was a silence lasting half a minute. Then rookie pitcher Al Schacht spoke up: "I'll pitch it, Griff." Griffith put his hand on Schacht's shoulder. "If you win this game today, Al, as long as I have anything to say about this ball club you'll have a job with me." Schacht won the game, 9–3, striking out Babe Ruth with the bases loaded for the final out. Schacht, who would later become known as the "Clown Prince of Baseball" when he took over Schaefer's spot as Nick Altrock's comedy partner, remembered Griffith's debt, asking for a job as a third base coach in 1924 and then claiming forever after that his arrival brought so much luck that the team won the World Series.

In the summer of 1920 a gruesome accident occurred that would change the game to the advantage of the batter. On August 16, Cleveland Indians shortstop Ray Chapman was at the plate in a game in New York when Yankee pitcher Carl Mays threw a fastball that hit him in the temple. The *Washington Star* described the scene: "So terrific was the blow that the report of the impact caused spectators to think the ball had struck his bat." The ball rolled halfway back to the pitcher's mound and Mays fielded it, not knowing what had happened. Chapman took two steps and collapsed.

He died shortly after. With him went all the advantages that pitchers had enjoyed: the ability to manipulate the ball at will with tobacco, saliva, gum, even an emery board. (Granddad once recalled that by the end of the game in the old days, the baseball looked like a lump of coal.) Trick pitches were now banned (exceptions were made for a few hurlers who couldn't pitch any other way), and umpires began to change balls frequently during the game.

These developments seemed to make a championship even more unlikely for Griffith's little ball club. Starting in 1920, hitting in the major leagues would explode, Ruth alone hitting 54 home runs that year. From 1900 to 1920 pitchers had won thirty games seventeen times; this would not happen once in the 1920s. Realizing that people paid to see the ball clubbed out of the park, owners made more adjustments. They lowered the pitcher's mound, shrank the strike zone and brought outfield fences in closer. Not everyone was happy with the changes, however. "Well, friends," Ring Lardner wrote in 1921, "may as well admit that I have kind of lose [*sic*] interest in the old game, or rather it ain't the old game which I have lose [*sic*] interest in, but it is the game which the managers have fixed up to please the public." Lardner lamented the rise of "the TNT Ball" and how it robbed scrappy old-style offensive players like Ty Cobb of "a chance to do things."

Major league batting averages in 1920 were almost thirty points higher than they had been in 1915. In 1915 there were nine .300 hitters; in 1927 there were thirty-five. Home runs went from 384 in 1915 to 631 in 1920, then shot up to over 1,000 in 1925. The number of .400 hitters doubled from four to eight between 1920 and 1930. There were half as many stolen bases in the 1920s as in the previous decade.

Another portentous change was that owners began to exercise greater authority over their players to keep the game honest. On September 27, 1920, just weeks after the death of Ray Chapman, a Philadelphia newspaper broke the news that for months had only been a rumor: the 1919 Chicago White Sox had thrown the World Series. The league appointed a commissioner to oversee and ensure the honesty of the game. Their choice was Kenesaw Mountain Landis, an imposing figure and not a man to cross.

A high school dropout, Landis had become a federal judge in Chicago, where he earned a reputation for being opinionated, vindictive and egotistical. He had a poor grasp of the law, but crusaded against anything he saw as radical or un-American. When a German submarine sank the *Lusitania* in 1915, Landis issued a legal summons on Kaiser Wilhelm. He then declared that in wartime, free speech "ceases," and he convicted over one hundred members of the Industrial Workers of the World, sentencing socialist leader Victor Berger to twenty years in prison and announcing that his only regret was that he couldn't have the prisoner shot. Landis's hair was snow white, and in every photograph I have ever seen of him he is scowling. Despite being a well-known moralizer—he was for Prohibition—he could curse like one of the players he watched over. (Once while helping his wife, Winifred, out of a taxi, Landis famously said, "Be careful, dear, or you'll break your goddam neck.") One of Landis's first official acts was to forbid players from fraternizing with fans, which led to the hundreds of dollars in fines imposed on Joe Judge whenever he was in New York and said hello to Bud Hannah, the mailman who had bought him his first baseman's mitt.

In Washington, it was my grandfather who had first tipped off Clark Griffith to the fact that the 1919 Series had been fixed. One day Joe went to the racetrack—a place, according to sportswriter Francis Stann, of which he was "inordinately fond"—where a friend told him that the Series had been bought by gangsters. When Granddad first reported the news, Griffith dismissed it with one word: "Nonsense!" Later on, after the news broke, Griffith changed his mind. "You were right, Joe," he said. "It was a bag job."

THE NEW AGE

In what would become a famous essay, Virginia Woolf wrote that "in or about December 1910, human character changed.... All human relations ... shifted." She was referring to the revolutionary change wrought by an exhibition of post-Impressionist paintings in London. The effect of the exhibit was so concussive, Woolf held, that it wiped out everything before it.

The same could be said of the changes that came over American culture at this time. The Victorian age was dissolving in the excitement generated by revolutionary scientific discoveries and technologies and the burgeoning entertainment and consumer culture. Ragtime was being played in the saloons and Irving Berlin was the country's great popular music composer, offering a vigor and spirit that could compete with, if not surpass, his more somber counterparts in Europe. With mass immigration, the population of the United States went from 76 million to 106 million during the second decade of the century, and average annual incomes climbed from $500 in 1900 to $1,500 by 1920.

Culturally, the 1920s were perhaps the most interesting decade of the twentieth century. It was a time when everything seemed to be expanding—cities, roads, moral boundaries. America was being transformed from a rural to an urban society, as armies of people flocked to cities to shake off what one writer called "the dead hand of the past."

Radio was becoming a dominant medium. (The 1924 World Series was one of the first to be broadcast to a national audience.) The first coast-to-coast airplane flight took place in 1923. Henry Ford's automobile revolution was remapping the country and making it mobile; between 1918 and 1931 the number of cars in New York City alone went from 185,000 to over 740,000. It was the dawn of the advertising age and mass media. By the end of the 1920s one out of three Americans regularly listened to the radio and three out of four went to the movies at least once a week. The new media culture made celebrities out of actors, singers and athletes.

The 1920s was also a time when America found itself in the middle of what a later age might have called a "culture war." Many people, disillusioned by the brutality and devastation of World War I—and encouraged by the postwar bohemians who formed a Lost Generation—rebelled against the Victorian ethos, which they saw as authoritarian, hypocritical and life-denying. The votaries of the past found themselves under challenge. In 1922, T. S. Eliot published "The Waste Land," a work that "abolished the idea of poetry for ladies," according to James Joyce. That same year Joyce published *Ulysses,* which claimed that history was a nightmare from which individuals had to awaken to liberate themselves. Rebellion against the past was the order of the day for writers and artists. Their enthusiastic defiance of convention was matched by their peers in other fields: Rudolf Valentino, Duke Ellington, Babe Ruth.

When Ruth came to play for the New York Yankees in 1920, he seemed to embody the dissident spirit of the 1920s and of New York itself, the capital of jazz, sexuality and every other lure of the new age. In the same way that modernism expanded the frontiers of art and personal behavior, Ruth redefined baseball. In 1919 he achieved the unthinkable when he hit 29 home runs. In 1920 he followed with 54, a figure at that time almost beyond imagining. Fans loved it: attendance at Yankee Stadium doubled between 1919 and 1920. (The 1920 mark of 1,789,472 customers was a record until the Yankees themselves beat it in 1946.) Ruth's $10,000 salary was doubled in 1920, then tripled in 1921. In 1922 he signed a five-year deal for an unheard-of $52,000 a year.

Ruth was a gigantic talent and an outsized personality who was tuned into the sensual rhythms of the new age. "The route to the common man's heart is paved with ribaldry and excess," baseball historian Harold Seymour wrote of Ruth's hold on fans. "What English king was more famous than Henry VIII?" One reporter described Ruth as "just a great, big, overgrown boy. He loves a good time, and ... there are always scores of admirers on hand to see that he does not suffer any pangs of ennui." In her memoir *My Dad the Babe,* Dorothy Ruth Pirone later recalled one of her father's archetypal moments. He had purchased, for cash, a sleek new Packard in Boston. On the drive back to New York he had a bad accident that totaled the car, though Ruth was able to climb through the driver's side window unscathed. He then hitchhiked to the next town, where he bought another Packard and finished the drive to New York.

Ruth was a rock star before rock and roll—or maybe characterizing him as a rapper *avant la lettre,* with that genre's fetish for cash and women, might be even more appropriate. He brokered the marriage between athletics and showbiz that would grow into the indissoluble union that it is today. As historian Ann Douglas observes in her book *Terrible Honesty: Mongrel Manhattan in the 1920s,*

> Sports was annexed by the burgeoning entertainment industry of the 1920s, and the man most responsible for their transformation was Babe Ruth, "our national exaggeration," as the sports writer Bill McGeehan called him. "All or nothing," was his motto, and he epitomized the "watch me—I'm a wow!" ethos. The Babe endorsed everything from baseball cards to cigars and cars.

Harold Seymour observes that the nickname "Sultan of Swat" was particularly appropriate for Ruth, "because Sultan applied to him off the field as well." Ruth frequented high-priced brothels and always had a suite stuffed with Prohibition liquor and beer. He took his pick of girls—often choosing more than one—and then sent everyone else out of the room. Whenever the Yankees went on a spring exhibition tour, a gaggle of females were at the train station to see the Babe off. "So long girls!" he would bawl. "See you next spring!"

Ruth displayed a raw aggressiveness that put an end to the image of the suave baseball player exemplified in the past by such performers as Christy Mathewson and Cap Anson, men who took pride in the knightly ideal of being *sans peur et sans reproche*. Fearless Ruth may have been, but he was far from being beyond reproach. As his cyclonic outburst during the Senators game in 1917 proved, he could be violent towards umpires. In June 1922 there was another episode that led to a letter of reprimand from American League president Ban Johnson, who chastised Ruth for "shameful and abusive language" towards an umpire. In 1925 he was fined a record $5,000 "for drinking and a lot of other things besides," according to Yankees manager Miller Huggins. "They don't fine bootleggers $5,000," the Babe sulked, "and men get out of murder charges for less."

At the time, and even to this day, sportswriters and fans wanted to see Ruth as a Horatio Alger figure, a ghetto-to-glory success story that reveals what's best about the American Dream. But as Harold Seymour notes:

> Ruth's life was that of a Horatio Alger hero insofar as it depicted the familiar climb from a lonely boyhood state to adult success. But there the parallel ends. Unlike the Alger heroes, Ruth did not struggle upward laboriously by dint of hard work and patient penny pinching, and his way of life was foreign to their stuffy, moralistic code. Indeed it may be that Ruth owed much of his tremendous popular appeal precisely to his flouting of the earlier code [and] probably attracted masses of people who wished subconsciously that they were free and courageous enough to cast aside social restrictions the way he did.

Perhaps Ruth was not so much a modern as what Aldous Huxley called a "contemporary ancient." In an interesting essay entitled, "What, Exactly, Is Modern?" in the May 1925 *Vanity Fair*, the future author of *Brave New World* describes meeting an Italian medical student at a café in Sienna. The student boasted of his sexual conquests of Siennese women, who, he said, "[were] really very modern." Huxley, who was far from being a prude, was quite put off by the young man's use of this term in the context of sexual promiscuity. His objection was that the term "modern" was typically used by artists as "the excuse for leading an idle, sordid, and perfectly useless life." With trademark intellectual brio, Huxley turns the tables:

> [A promiscuous person] is not modern, but on the contrary, antique and atavistic. To behave like the Romans under Caracalla, the Asiatic Greeks, the Babylonians, is not a bit modern. In point of historical fact it is monogamy, love and chastity that are the modern inventions. My Italian friend [and those like him] were terribly old-fashioned, if only they had known it. They were eighteenth-century in their outlook, they were Roman empire, they were Babylonian.

Then—after denouncing "modern" art (it apes primitive art but has no deep spiritual meaning) and James Joyce's *Ulysses* ("simply the reaction of its author against his medieval Catholic education")—Huxley comes up with his striking phrase: "contemporary ancients."

Babe Ruth could have been the king of contemporary ancients, with New York as his throne. New York's population doubled between 1910 and 1930. The new inhabitants included Thomas Wolfe, John Dos Passos, Paul Robeson, F. Scott and Zelda Fitzgerald, Harry Houdini, Daymon Runyon, Duke Ellington and Langston Hughes. The last two were refugees from Washington, D.C., then perceived as a small, conservative southern town. Indeed, how could tiny Washington compete with New York, in baseball or any other way? As Ann Douglas puts it,

> America is the only western nation whose capital city is a kind of showcased national toy. With its laid out avenues, its stately replication of monuments, its uniform quasi-classical architectural manner, Washington seems deliberately antithetical to New York's stylistically jumbled assemblage of buildings

and chaotic profusion of commercial enterprises, all advertising New York's, and America's, ethnically and racially diverse population.

New York was also home to the best baseball teams in America, the Yankees and the Giants. The Giants won the World Series in 1921, and that same year Babe Ruth had his best year up to that time: 59 home runs, a .378 average, 119 extra-base hits, 177 runs and 171 RBIs, along with 17 stolen bases, a slugging average of .846 and 457 total bases. The Giants took the Series again in 1922. Ruth answered for the Yankees the following year by taking the Series from the Giants. Ruth hit a career high .393, which included 41 homers, 131 RBIs and 395 total bases. Babe's power typified the new kind of baseball—jazz age baseball—that the Senators with their slap hitters were ill-equipped to play.

Even if the Senators could somehow get past the Yankees and win a pennant, they would probably have to face the Giants, who were favored to take a fourth pennant in 1924. The Giants had several stars, among them right fielder Ross Youngs, who batted .357 in 1921. In the seventh inning of the 1921 World Series, Youngs became the first player to get two hits in a single inning, sparking an eight-run rally. The Giants repeated as champions in 1922 with an infield that consisted of three future Hall of Famers—George Kelly at first, Frankie Frisch at second and Dave Bancroft at short. At third base was Heinie Groh, who still holds the National League record for fielding.

The Giants' captain was Frankie Frisch, "the Fordham Flash." The son of a wealthy New York linen manufacturer, Frisch attended Fordham University, where he captained the football, basketball and baseball teams. He was an all-American halfback before joining the Giants in 1919, and would be McGraw's pet and prodigy until the two had a celebrated falling-out in 1926. Frisch hit .328 in 1924 and beat out Rogers Hornsby for the league lead in runs with 121.

Behind all these men was manager John McGraw. In his twenty-two years with the Giants, McGraw won ten pennants, eight second-place finishes and three World Series titles.

Although called baseball's Little Napoleon, he had more in common with Rockefeller, Carnegie and other empire builders.

If Washington seemed a baseball backwater compared with New York, however, the nation's capital had more in common with New York culturally. Washington in the 1920s was a bustling and in some ways innovative city. To be sure, it was, as its stodgy reputation suggested, a town of marble columns and alabaster floors, of smoke-filled political backrooms and early bedtimes. But in addition to this public face there was another Washington: a steamy, energetic place of row houses, bars, movie palaces (some of the grandest in the nation), dances, parks, immigrants, Prohibition liquor, debutantes, clanging streetcars and tireless construction. After a slump in 1921, the D.C. economy roared back, and the city underwent vast and seemingly endless growth. Hotels, office buildings, giant department stores like Hecht's went up, as did three thousand new trees planted by the park service. Contractors purchased entire blocks to put up new houses. In 1925, investments in new buildings would reach $63 million, a staggering sum in those days.

As in New York, traffic congestion became a problem. The number of drivers would reach more than 170,000 in 1930—this in a city of only about 500,000 people. "The entire Mall has become an open-air garage," wrote one protestor. "On the Department of Agriculture grounds automobiles are parked on the grass."

Washington's social and intellectual life was always vibrant, even if not as avant-garde or glamorous as New York's; it was a city of dinner parties, hotel dances, teas and social clubs; and it was the home of the Smithsonian Institution and the National Research Council, which offered fellowships and grants in eleven fields, including psychology, anthropology, geology and medicine. There were also the American Council on Education, the American Council of Learned Societies devoted to "humanistic sciences," and of course the Library of Congress. All of this was surrounded by neighborhoods of brightly colored row houses, saloons, gardens and parks and children playing in the streets.

One historian noted that the Washington of the 1920s was assumed to be "the most temporary society in America" because of incoming and outgoing politicians, but it was actually a permanent home to thousands of immigrants, teachers, journalists, war veterans and widows. Constance Green wrote of the period:

> Frequently startled to find such diversity, the discerning newcomer was invariably struck by Washington's persistent village-like quality. Its unexpectedness entranced most people. Here was a bucolic Cleopatra whose wiles seduced the citizen. World capital though she was, the chief official personages who people the scene are villagers with a villager's attitude and a villager's background.

One recollection of daily life in Washington came from Anita Judge, Joe Judge's daughter and my aunt, who died in 2002. Anita always remembered riding the trolley to American League Park (later Griffith Stadium) down Seventh Street from her Petworth house, along the way passing neither monuments, government offices nor orators heading for Capitol Hill, but rather restaurants, churches and, most memorably, a gigantic building that took up an entire block next to the stadium. It was the Bond Bakery, and Anita knew she was getting near the ball park when she smelled the bread.

Washington even had a village within a village, with Griffith Stadium occupying its very center. This was the neighborhood known as Shaw (a name not formally acquired until the 1960s), one of the most remarkable African-American enclaves in the country. Abutting the stadium on one side was Howard University, which had become one of the outstanding black colleges in the nation after opening in 1867. On another side was Freedman's Hospital, the only hospital for blacks in the segregated city. Running past the stadium was U Street, known as the "Black Broadway" because it was the home of over three hundred black-owned businesses, including theaters, dance halls and cabarets. A partial list of Shaw's businesses from 1910 shows the variety: E. R. Pusseli's Insurance, Loan and Real Estates; Milton M. Holland's Life Insurance Company; Virginia Industrial Mercantile Building and Loan Association; the Capital Savings Bank, one of the first black-owned banks in the country.

And there were theaters like the Republic, the Booker T., the Lincoln, the Dunbar, and the Howard, the oldest black-owned theater in America. After the show people went dancing at places like Lincoln Colonnade, Murray's Casino or the Prince Hall Lodge, at nightclubs like the Crystal Caverns (decorated inside like a cave), then to after-hours spots such as Cecilia's and the Cimmarron. And Shaw abounded with lawyers, dentists, printers and painters, as well as six drugstores, four of which were owned and operated by women.

To the immediate north of U Street and Griffith Stadium was LeDroit Park, one of the best middle- and upper-class black neighborhoods in America. Many of the residents in Shaw went to Dunbar High School, an all-black institution whose students often did better on standardized tests than those in the white community.

A trolley line followed Seventh Street, a main artery through Shaw, starting at the Capitol building and running up long, low hills until it stopped in front of Griffith Stadium. Another trolley line ran up Fourteenth Street, which also connected Shaw with downtown. Griffith Stadium lay at the heart of black Washington, in the geographical and often in the emotional sense.

Blacks in Washington were proud and defensive of Shaw. During the Red Scare of 1919, race riots erupted in the capital and other cities. In the District, the city exploded when it was reported that a black man had raped several white females. Whites came to Shaw looking for blood, prodded by the shamelessly racist *Washington Post,* but found resistance when they were met by a group of two thousand armed black men carrying weapons distributed to them on the corner of Seventh and U, right next to the ball park.

The famous black poet Langston Hughes, who lived in Washington briefly in the 1920s and worked in a restaurant where he was called "the busboy poet," loved the "color" of Seventh Street. He referred to the strip as the place where "they played the blues, ate watermelon, barbeque, and fish sandwiches, shot pool, told tall tales, looked at the dome of the Capitol and laughed out loud." He might have added, "and argued about baseball," for Griffith Stadium was one of the few public places in Washington that was desegregated, and the city's blacks felt that the Senators were their team.

Hughes would set many of his poems along Seventh Street, even after he moved to New York in 1927. His departure was part of a larger trend of black talent going north for recognition.

Black Washington was deeply conservative—one writer referred to it as "a city of Babbitts, both black and white." There was a culture war going on in the 1920s, within both black and white Washington society, between those who favored open embrace of contemporary mores and those who defended older traditions. Kelly Miller, the chairman of the sociology department at Howard University, was of the latter party. He took to task a 1926 book about the Harlem Renaissance, called *Nigger Heaven:*

> [It is] merely an artistic portrayal of the Harlem Negro, in his gayer mood for joy and jazz.... The Negro life in Harlem is mainly effervescence and froth without seriousness or solid supporting basis. The riot of frolic and frivolity is characteristic of Babylon on the verge of destruction rather than that of Heaven, the blissful abode of tradition.

Many artists of the Harlem Renaissance had connections to Washington; it could even be argued that the Renaissance might not have been possible without the city. In 1925 Alain Locke, the first black Rhodes scholar and a professor at Howard University, edited a special "Harlem Issue" of the magazine *Survey Graphic.* The issue, which sold 40,000 copies, was published in Washington. That same year Locke edited *The New Negro,* a compilation of plays, short stories and essays by black writers that became the manifesto of the Harlem Renaissance. Of the thirty-five contributors, sixteen had affiliations with Washington, either by birth, education or work.

In the end, however, many could not resist the attractions of culturally experimental New York, so different from the buttoned-down conservatism of black Washington. Perhaps the greatest artistic loss was Duke Ellington, who played his first jazz gig at the True Reformers Hall a couple of blocks down from Griffith Stadium. Ellington wanted to be a baseball player, and sold hotdogs at the ball park when he was growing up. But he left for New York in 1923. He was followed by a host of young black writers: Jean Toomer, who had been a manager at the Howard Theater and would write *Cane,* a famous novel of the Harlem Renaissance; Albert Rice; and Langston Hughes. In 1927, Hughes wrote:

> I have seen Washington, a city of which I have heard much, and I have looked at something called "society," of which I have heard much, too. Now I can live in Harlem where people are not so ostentatiously proud of themselves, and where one's family background is not of such great concern.

Besides Griffith Stadium, the only desegregated places in Washington were the trolleys and the Library of Congress. Although in 1920 a black man, Rube Foster, had created the Negro League, Washington would not have a black team play in Griffith for years, until Pennsylvania's Homestead Grays made arrangements to play there in the 1930s. In 1927 William H. Jones, a sociology professor at Howard University, gave a backhanded compliment to the Senators in his book *Recreation and Amusement among Negroes in Washington, D.C.:*

> Perhaps in few other cities does baseball hold such an insignificant place among colored people as it does in Washington. No prominent Negro team exists. Some baseball is played, however, by the Y.M.C.A. teams, but such games are of minor importance. It seems that the big-league games have so enlisted the Washington Negroes' interest and loyalty that no enthusiasm can be aroused for such a game among themselves.... The colored citizens devoutly rally to the local American League club. Here, as in no other phase of their recreational life, contacts between the races suffer less restrictions. In the American League Baseball Park there is comparatively no conscious segregation and the races mingle freely.

Jones went on to observe that when the Senators went to the World Series in 1924,

> [I]n the lines during the rush for ... tickets all social distances were violated and even forgotten. The "fans" of both races

vied with each other in the same line.... Hot coffee, sandwiches, and "hot dogs" were bought by the famished "lineholders" from whomever chanced to come their way, irrespective of race and nationality.

That year the *Daily American,* a newspaper for Washington's black community, declared: "Long live King Baseball, the only monarch who recognizes no color line."

In another book, Jones and co-author Damon P. Young accused Senators management of making it harder for black fans to get tickets through the mail for the World Series. As a result, or so Jones and Young claimed, black enthusiasm for the Senators trailed off: "This incident lowered somewhat the morale of the Negro 'fans' and kept from the games many Negroes, who say they have been veteran supporters of the club—some ever since those days when it was scarcely more than a 'sand-lot' team, and when Walter Johnson's balls did not have quite so much 'smoke.'" The feeling was equally sour at the *Washington Tribune,* another black-owned paper: "We failed to get the kick out of the recent World Series that many of our fellow townsmen got," the paper editorialized on October 18, 1924. "To think that the doors of organized baseball are absolutely closed to colored ball players is enough to cause us to give our full time and support to [black] baseball, regardless of its class."

This frustration is expressed by Sam Lacy, one of the oldest and most distinguished living sportswriters in America. Born in 1903, Lacy came to Washington in 1905 and grew up on Thirteenth and U Street. He told me:

> We lived about six blocks from Griffith Stadium. Every morning we used to go over and chase batting practice for the Washington Nationals. They'd have practice at ten o'clock in the morning, and the kids would go over and practice and then we'd get in free to be vendors in the afternoon.

As a fan who watched Negro League games as well as the Senators, Lacy got to compare players. He soon concluded that Griffith's policy just "didn't make any sense." There were plenty of players in the Negro Leagues who could have helped Griffith win.

Some claimed that Griffith was a racist. It is probably more accurate to say that he was simply someone constrained by the mental habits of his time and a businessman who calculated that desegregating his team would make for fewer white customers in a city that was still in some ways a small southern town.

Griffith had evidence to back up his fears. In October of 1920, Joe Judge had organized a group of players, both Senators and minor-leaguers, to play an exhibition game against the Brooklyn Royal Giants, a black team, at Griffith Stadium. There was a close call at the plate that favored the Giants. The umpire who made the call was black, and Senators outfielder Frank Broner slugged him, causing a near-riot. None of the white Washington papers covered the melee, but the black ones did. I never found a statement by my grandfather about what happened, but the fact that he was a driving force behind the game indicates that he was ahead of his time on racial matters.

In fact, Griffith cared less about race than about winning. In 1934 he hired Joe Cambria as a scout, and was delighted when Cambria ignored the usual avenues for players and went to Latin America instead. Cambria had played minor league ball in Cuba and was impressed by the talent he had seen. In 1935 he signed Bobby Estalella from Havana; other Cubans to follow would be Rene Monteagudo, Alejandro Alexander Aparicio, Elroy Carraswuel and Roberto Oritiz.

There is even evidence that Griffith genuinely liked Josh Gibson and other Negro League stars and felt bad that he couldn't use them. Griffith often came to the Homestead Grays' games and stopped by the dugout. At one game he asked Gibson, "Are you going to hit a home run for me today?" Gibson obliged, hitting a ball to the top of a Briggs hotdog sign, high above the bleachers. According to one witness, "old man Griffith almost swallowed his cigar." (Mickey Mantle hit the longest major league ball at Griffith, a 565-foot blast that actually left the stadium and rolled into someone's front yard.) In 1942, when a Communist Party campaign called for the desegregation of the majors, Griffith invited Gibson and Buck Leonard, the two great stars of the Negro League, into his office. "If I take you boys," he told them, "it will break up your league." The Senators wouldn't break the color barrier until the mid-1950s.

$$\mathcal{O}$$

EVEN AS THE TEAM WAS losing games in the early 1920s, Clark Griffith was quietly building what would become his World Series team. He already had Sam Rice in the outfield and Joe Judge at first. Ironically, it was now the Senators' great star Walter Johnson who held the team back after carrying it for fifteen years. On May 7, 1921, Babe Ruth tagged a Walter Johnson pitch for what was then the longest ball hit out of Griffith Stadium. Johnson recalled the colossal shot in 1942:

> [Ruth] was in a terrible slump once, and I struck him out three times. But the fourth time he came up ... goodness, he hit that ball. It went over the fence and into a big tree across the alley. Colored fans used to pay 25 cents to sit on the limb of the tree, and it was packed this day. When Ruth's ball sailed into the tree, the fans fell out like apples.

One of the witnesses to the hit was former president Woodrow Wilson. Wilson was in ailing health and would die three years later; he watched the game from his sedan, which was parked behind the Senators' right-field bullpen.

On May 15, 1921, the 33-year-old Johnson, still recovering from a persistent cold (the Big Train would often be held back by colds), was taken out of a game in Detroit after giving up eight runs in four innings. When the Senators were trailing the Yankees and the Indians by just a few games in June, Johnson lost back-to-back games. During one, a 10–6 loss to the Tigers when Johnson was driven out in the fifth inning, the pitcher was actually booed. As a reporter observed:

> At first a few [booed], then a chorus, and soon it was the distressing yell of a mob, as Johnson, beaten, stood on the mound in the fifth. His delivery constantly slowed down. Normally a fast worker, he took more and more time between each pitch. Once he rubbed his glove hand across his eyes. It may have been a speck of dust that bothered his vision; it probably was a tear.

An editorial in the *Detroit News* claimed that "Washington is pennant crazy and, with this unaccustomed smell of battle in its nostrils, is ready to rend its own and devour those who, it thinks, hinder its progress."

Still, a bad year for Johnson would be a remarkable year for any other pitcher. He won seventeen games, and on September 5 he struck out seven Yankees, thereby breaking Cy Young's career record of 2,796. He led the major leagues in strikeouts, and his speed could still seem superhuman. In one game against the Athletics, Johnson threw so hard that one of the A's, Jimmy Dykes, said he "didn't even have time to think about swinging." In fact, he didn't even see the ball. After a pitch the umpire told Dykes to take his base. Dykes looked at the umpire incredulously. He hadn't felt anything. The umpire then asked him if he always wore his hat that way. Johnson's pitch had hit the brim, turning the cap halfway around. Al Schacht remarked that for the rest of the game the Athletics were "virtually taking their cuts from the dugout."

The Senators finished the 1921 season in fourth place. It was an improvement over previous years, but Washington was still an old-style ball club, emphasizing slap hits and fielding at a time when the game was evolving into a contest of brute batting power. The 1921 Senators hit .277; they were next to last in batting, with the Yankees blasting almost three times as many home runs. However, Joe Judge had a good year at the plate. He hit .301, and on August 9, during a nineteen-inning marathon with the Browns (who won), he hit three triples. It was an American League record for many years.

Granddad was now a mainstay of the team and the father of two young daughters, Catherine, who was born in 1917, and Anita, who arrived two years later. Joe may have had a genteel soul, but he had fallen in love with a rough game. On September 21 of the 1921 season, he was witness to a bloody brawl at Griffith Stadium between Ty Cobb and umpire Billy Evans. The Senators had downed the Tigers 5–1 and Cobb was outraged by what he saw as Evans's poor officiating. He challenged Evans to a fight, and the two men fought it out right under the grandstand, in full view of the fans, the players and Cobb's son Ty

Junior. An accomplished brawler, Cobb got the better of Evans. When the incident was reported to Commissioner Landis, he suspended Cobb.

This year would be devastating for Walter Johnson off the mound, too. The Senators were in St. Louis on July 9 when he got word that Frank, his 59-year-old father, was sick. Johnson left for the family home in Coffeyville, Kansas, but by the time he arrived it was too late: his father had died of a stroke. Johnson wouldn't return to the team for two weeks.

In the off season things would get even worse for him. Just before Christmas his two-and-a-half-year-old daughter Elinor died from influenza. Johnson found the loss almost unbearable. "Only people who have had the same experience know what it means to a home," he wrote later on.

After the death of the little girl, Johnson, his wife Hazel and their son Eddie all came down with the flu, and Hazel suffered an infection in her eye that required surgery. In 1922, for the first time in eleven years, Johnson wasn't on the mound for the Senators on Opening Day. He did get some cheer before the game, however. President Harding was in attendance, and while the teams warmed up he called six-year-old Eddie over to the president's box. He hoisted the boy on his knee, and at the end of the first inning Johnson emerged from the dugout to see where his son had gone. "That's a mighty fine boy you have there," Harding said after handing Johnson back his son.

Faced with tragedy, bad health and a mediocre team, Johnson may have thought of retiring. But he found letting go difficult. He later wrote:

> I used to say that I would finish while I was still good, that I would leave voluntarily instead of being forced out. But I am beginning to sympathize with the point of view of some of the old veterans that I have heard say they would quit only when they had their uniforms taken away by force.

Ŋ

AFTER THE 1921 SEASON ENDED, Griffith added three more players who dramatically increased Washington's strength. The first was left-handed slugger Leon "Goose" Goslin. While playing golf in the winter, Griffith heard that Jack Dunn, who ran a league in Baltimore, was about to buy Goslin, a sensational 20-year-old player from Columbia, South Carolina. Dunn had discovered Babe Ruth, and when Griffith got Goslin's name from his inform- ant, he stepped in and bought him for $6,000.

Like every other player in Washington, Goslin would not hit many home runs in Griffith Stadium, but he would send the ball just about everywhere else in the park. In an 18-year career he hit .316 with a .500 slugging average. He drove in 100 or more RBIs in eleven seasons. Goslin was cocky and loved a good time. He was a sharp dresser—my aunt Anita remembered pearl but- tons on his shirt—and he had what one writer described as an "ample" nose that invited comparisons to Jimmy Durante's. He used a closed batting stance, and once joked that he would have batted .500 if he could have seen over his nose.

At his debut for the Senators, Goslin hit the ball well against Boston's Red Faber, a future Hall of Famer who was completing a 25-win season. When he scored and got back to the bench, Joe Judge said he never thought he'd see the day the Senators had as big a lead over the Red Sox. Goslin replied that he actually didn't think this Faber guy was any good at all.

Goose Goslin was devoid of any guile or pretentiousness. With the perspective of years, he wryly said about himself:

> Heck, let's face it, I was just a big ol' country boy havin' the time of his life. It was all a lark to me, just a joy ride. Never feared a thing, never got nervous, just a big country kid from South Jersey, too dumb to know better. In those days I'd go out and fight a bull without a sword and never know the dif- ference. . . . It was just a game, that's all it was.

Goose was, as one writer put it, "a manager's nightmare"—or, as the *Washington Post* referred to him, "Washington's answer to Babe Ruth." Two weeks into 1922 spring training, he stayed out all night gambling, going, as one writer noted, "directly from the craps table to the breakfast table." There he ran into his man- ager, Clyde Milan. (Former manager George McBride had suf- fered a nervous breakdown in August after his face was partially paralyzed by a thrown ball, and outfielder Milan was forced to take over.) Milan in short order sent him back to his room to get some sleep; an hour later, evidently suspecting something of the sort, he checked out Goose's room, only to find the madcap young batter decamped: he had escaped through an open window.

Griffith's second acquisition in the off season was Roger Peckinpaugh, a bowlegged 31-year-old veteran shortstop. "Peck" had been the Yankees' shortstop since 1914, and had been a key player in the team's pennant win of 1921. But then he had been traded to Boston in a deal by Red Sox owner Harry Frazee. Part of the reason for the trade was that Babe Ruth, finishing his first season with the Yankees, had openly campaigned for Peckinpaugh to take over as manager for the Yankees, and the team's owners, content with manager Miller Huggins, sent Peck to Boston as a reproach to Ruth for his overreaching. Peckinpaugh never even had a chance to suit up for the Red Sox before he was sold to Washington for $50,000.

It was money well spent on Griffith's part. Peck was the premier shortstop in the majors, and together with Harris and Judge would form one of the greatest double-play combinations in baseball history. (Griffith once said of them, "When the ball is hit in their direction, everybody is out.") In 1922, the trio would combine for 168 double plays, and many thought them superior to the Cubs' more famous Tinker, Evers and Chance.

Rounding out the infield was a 21-year-old sandlot star from Chicago, Oscar "Ossie" Bluege. He would play eighteen years in the majors and was considered one of the best third basemen of his day. Griffith in his later years called him "the greatest fielder I ever saw," even insisting that he was better than the Baltimore Orioles' Brooks Robinson. Bluege played his position shallower than any other third baseman, reasoning that the ground he had to cover was cone-shaped, and that playing closer to home meant "cutting the angles." Luckily he had the reflexes to nab shots before they got into the outfield. Bluege resembled Johnson and Judge—quiet, humble and soft-spoken—"poker-faced with a golden glove," as one writer put it. The expert scout, Joe Engel, almost passed on Bluege when he checked him out late in 1921; Bluege had injured his knee. But Engel, with his unique methods, challenged the ballplayer to a footrace. Ossie beat the scout with ease and signed his contract that night.

Even with the new players, the Senators would finish in sixth place in 1922, with Goslin their only .300 hitter. Once again the Giants beat the Yankees in the World Series, with McGraw relying on his formula of a five-star infield, steady pitching and a long-hitting left fielder he had signed in 1921, Emil "Irish" Meusel. While McGraw focused on the fundamentals of the old game he had grown up playing, the game of stolen bases and strategy, George Sisler, the 1922 American League Most Valuable Player, was hitting .420. (In 1924, Rogers Hornsby would achieve the highest batting average of the century, .424.)

Although the Yankees returned to the World Series in 1922, Babe Ruth had one of the worst slumps of his career. That year he was suspended by Commissioner Landis for making money barnstorming in the off season, an activity forbidden to World Series players. He hadn't gotten into a game until May 20, when he went 0–4 and was loudly booed by fans. In June a fight with another umpire cost him another suspension. By the time of the World Series, Ruth had batted .315 in 110 games with 35 home runs. Nevertheless, at a postseason dinner Jimmy Walker, the future mayor of New York, shamed the Babe by saying he had let down the "dirty-faced kids" who idolized him.

Hurt, Ruth retreated to his farm in Sudbury, Massachusetts; but the criticism of others spurred him to prepare for 1923, and he lost 20 pounds. On Opening Day 1923, he hit a home run against the Red Sox, to the delight of a record 70,000 fans in the new Yankees Stadium—already being called "The House That Ruth Built." That year he would hit a career high .393 and lead the circuit in homers, RBIs, slugging and total bases. The Yankees won the pennant—they were sixteen games ahead of Ty Cobb's Tigers—and then the World Series. There seemed little doubt that New York—both New Yorks—would be back for the 1924 World Series.

In 1923 the Senators went 75–78 and finished fourth. Even worse, their workhorse seemed to be showing signs of age. On May 20, 1923, Walter Johnson, now thirty-five years old, hurt his left knee while pitching in St. Louis, an injury that would bother him all season. There were only a few bright spots during this season, one being a 4–3 victory over the Yankees before a capacity crowd in the first Sunday game ever played in Yankee Stadium.

Despite the Senators' poor performance, interest in the team was high, at least compared with previous years. The attendance figure of 360,000 at Griffith Stadium in 1923 was twice as high as in 1919, the year Griffith had taken over as owner. Fans appreciated that Griffith plowed a lot of their money back into the team. In 1923 he added 13,000 seats to the stadium, renovated the clubhouses and resodded the field, making it, according to some, the best diamond in the league.

Griffith also kept adding players to his roster. One was outfielder Nemo Leibold, who hit .305 in 1923. Another was catcher Herold "Muddy" Ruel. A practicing attorney who had graduated from Washington University Law School, Ruel was "the only big-league catcher certified to practice before the United States Supreme Court," as writer Shirley Povich put it. Only 5'9" and 150 pounds, by the end of the grueling 1924 season he would be down to 130 pounds, catching in all but five of the Senators' 154 games. He didn't have the most powerful arm in the league, but was a tough clutch hitter and brilliant at calling pitches. Before Yankees manager Miller Huggins died in 1929, he was asked if he had ever been mistaken about a player. Yes, he replied, he had once let Muddy Ruel go.

In sixteen years in the majors, there wasn't a time—or at least one that was recorded—when Ruel lost his temper. If he disagreed with an umpire's call he would simply shake his head, at most muttering "I thought that pitch was all right." Instead of tobacco, he chewed gum. The worst he would call someone was a "rogue," and when a player took the Lord's name in vain Ruel would say, "Why don't you call on someone you know?" He also liked books, which allowed the other players to razz him. He had to smuggle volumes into his room for fear of being found out. Yet the players also respected him, giving him a position of authority to settle arguments and deal with problems between them.

As a boy growing up in St. Louis, Ruel had idolized Walter Johnson, always trying to see Johnson play at Sportsman's Park when the Senators were in town. St. Louis was also where "Muddy" had acquired his nickname, bestowed when he splattered himself while batting a muddy baseball. Ruel had joined the St. Louis Browns at nineteen. He didn't make an impression his first year, and spent the next two years in the minors. After serving in World War I, Ruel was bought up by the Red Sox, where he had two outstanding seasons in 1921 and 1922. When Ruel got to the Senators in 1923 he heard rumors that his idol Johnson, now in his mid-thirties, was past his prime. Ruel spent hours working with Johnson, encouraging him and convincing him that, even as a brilliant fastball pitcher, he could mix up his pitches and get more out of his arm. In 1923 Johnson went 17–12, his best year since 1919.

Late in the 1923 season, Joe Engel made another discovery, a 25-year-old pitcher from Texas named Fred Marberry. At 6'1" and 200 pounds, Marberry was nicknamed "Firpo" because of his resemblance to the Argentine boxer Luis Firpo. Marberry would be the first great relief pitcher in the majors, a man whose sole job was to come in late in the game and preserve a victory. Marberry thought that the role of a reliever was a lesser position, and was always eager to prove himself. As Al Schacht once recalled, "Sometimes [the manager] would go to the pitcher's mound just to talk to the pitcher, unsure about whether or not to take him out. But he'd no sooner get to the mound, and there would be Marberry—out of the bullpen, coming in. He was that willing and that anxious." And Ossie Bluege observed, "You should have seen Fred walk across the outfield when he was coming in to relieve. He moved just as fast as he could and just as determined and as confident as could be." It took him only about six pitches to warm up.

Fred Marberry never backed down from a fight. At a game in New York the Yankees were teasing him endlessly. After the game, he was passing the Yankees' bench and stopped. "You, Ruth, can be the first," he called to the New York star. "And you'll need all the help you can round up." The Yankees just stared at him in silence, and neither Ruth nor anyone else took him up on his offer of a fight.

Fans were pleased with the new acquisitions—that is, until Griffith made a choice for a new manager: the 27-year-old second baseman Bucky Harris. Harris had been made team captain in 1923, but he—along with everyone else—was stunned when he got the offer. In fact, up until then Harris thought he was in the doghouse with the owner for having played basketball in the off season to make extra money, a violation of the Senators' rules. (Harris had gotten a black eye in one game and then was spotted by Griffith's secretary at a New Year's Eve party.)

Instead, while he was in Tampa getting ready for spring training, Harris received a letter from Griffith: "If you want the job, it's yours." Harris tried to call Griffith to accept, but the connection was bad. So he gave the Western Union man $20 and told him to keep sending the same telegram for four hours: "I'll take that job and win Washington's first American League pennant."

Except for Goose Goslin, Harris was the youngest player on the team. Sportswriters immediately dubbed the selection "Griffith's Folly."

ASCENT OF THE SENATORS

Bucky Harris's first act as manager was to go to veterans Joe Judge, now thirty-one, and Walter Johnson, thirty-six, both of whom he thought might have resented being passed over for the position, to ask for their support. Both men gave it unconditionally. "The boys all like Harris and are going to work hard for him," Johnson told the press. Harris stopped doing bed checks and cut down on other authoritarian restrictions as a sign that he trusted his players. At Hot Springs, Arkansas, where the Senators went for a kind of pre-spring training, the men began to bond. They played cards and golf, took hikes and worked out together. Harris later claimed that Hot Springs was "the foundation for the club spirit which helped carry us to success."

It was also the foundation of a spectacular prank played on Al Schacht. The pitcher's career had supposedly ended in 1921, but he had hoped to make the team again in 1924. (He would get a coaching job instead.) Schacht had a particularly close friendship with Walter Johnson; when Johnson had trouble with his arm in the 1920 season—the year Schacht had to come in and pitch and creamed the Yankees—Schacht often cheered him with comedy routines, doing pantomime and arguing over their favorite card game, casino. When doctors told Johnson in 1920 that the pain in his arm was just temporary, then informed Schacht that his own arm was shot, it was

Johnson's turn to cheer up his friend. The two men would be road trip roommates for seven years.

Schacht was in Tampa when the Senators arrived for training in the spring of 1924. He was up to his old routines, which in the future would make him the "Clown Prince of Baseball," playing to audiences before and during games in ballparks all over the country. For the crowd in the lobby of the Tampa Hotel he did a mean imitation of Johnson, right down to what Johnson's grandson called his "Will Rogers-like 'aw-shucks' mannerisms." In reply, Johnson called Schacht "Jack Keefe," the name of a third-rate pitcher in Ring Lardner's book *You Know Me Al.*

One day in Tampa, Bucky Harris told Schacht that while the team was in Hot Springs they had met "a couple of the most beautiful women I have ever seen." Harris had told the ladies all about Al Schacht, he said, and they were dying to meet him. In fact, they were arriving in a few days and renting a cottage in the country. He should go out there and ask for Margie.

A few days later Schacht got a haircut and a shave, put on his best suit and bought a bottle of Prohibition liquor and a dozen oranges. It was dark when the cab dropped off Schacht and Harris at the cabin. Harris knocked on the door and a man answered. Schacht asked for Margie.

Then, as Schacht later described it, "in one brief moment the peace of the night was shattered." The man at the door pulled out a revolver and pointed it at Harris. "So you're the dirty bums who are trying to break up my home!" he yelled, firing two shots. Harris collapsed off the porch as if hit. "And now I'll get you, you rat!" the man shouted at Schacht.

As a volley of shots rang out, Schacht sprang off the porch, tearing down the road towards the team hotel back in Tampa. He ran, then walked, then ran again, hiding behind bushes whenever a car passed. He could barely walk by the time he got back to the lobby. "You look a little pale, Al," one of the Senators said. Then the whole squad, including Harris, appeared, erupting in laughter. The entire thing had been a setup. Players had been in the bushes outside the house, many with guns they shot in the air as Schacht fled. "What really hurts," Schacht would recall years later, "is that they couldn't keep it to themselves. Even now every once in a while someone will shout, 'Hey, Al, how's Tampa Margie?'" (One of the men in the bushes had been Walter Johnson, although he was laughing too hard to fire his pistol.)

In 1924 Johnson felt that he had largely healed from the injuries of the early 1920s, and wrote in a newspaper column, "I am in fine shape, never felt better in my life and expect to have a better season than the last one." After seeing his first workout, Harris said, "I can't imagine Walter ever having been faster than he is right now." Yet Johnson was thirty-six, and he had said that 1924 would be his last season. However well his arm felt, it wasn't what it once had been. Where his cannon used to recharge quickly, allowing him to pitch both ends of a doubleheader, now he felt he could only pitch every four days. Johnson knew what had happened to him. In the summer of 1924, when the Senators were in the thick of the pennant chase, he would tell *Baseball* magazine:

> My principal regret this season is the knowledge that I am not what I used to be as pitcher. If I could have the strength and speed and endurance that I knew ten years back, this pennant would be in and I don't mean to be at all boastful in making that statement. I know what I used to do with a losing ball club and I know well enough what I could do now with such a club as we have behind me. If the old right arm was young, I could pitch every other day from now on till the pennant was ours, and I wouldn't lose any games either.... If only I could be for one short month the pitcher I used to be!

Johnson would lead the league with 38 starts in 1924, but would only finish 20 of them. Fred Marberry saved five of the Big Train's wins.

✺

FEW OBSERVERS THOUGHT THE SENATORS would amount to much in 1924. On March 23, *Washington Star* sportswriter John B. Keller made a prediction about the team: they would stink. Keller went through the lineup, emphasizing the defects of the roster:

outfielders Nemo Leibold, Goslin and Rice; infielders Harris, Peckinpaugh, Judge and Bluege; catcher Muddy Ruel and pitchers Walter Johnson and George Mogridge. This group was "not so different from the team used during the later part of the last season," which had finished in fourth, seven games behind the third-place Indians. The only reason the Senators hadn't done worse, wrote Keller, was that their last games had been against the "hapless, last-place Red Sox."

Most writers thought that the World Series would again be between the two great New York teams. In early 1924 the Giants had added a pivotal player to their already sterling roster, future Hall of Fame first baseman Bill Terry. Terry had grown up in Memphis and dropped out of school at fifteen to work in a railroad yard, then went into the oil business where he was discovered by McGraw. From the start, Terry was one of the few players not fazed by McGraw. When the Giants manager met Terry to talk about playing for the Giants, the manager went on at length about what an honor it was to be a member of the New York Giants. McGraw then suggested that Terry sign a contract.

"For how much?" Terry asked.

It was a question no one had ever asked him before. McGraw had to haggle with Terry before settling on $5,000. In the years to come, the two men frequently did battle, about contracts and everything else. Once, when he came upon Little Napoleon berating a player, Terry said, "You've been blaming other people for the mistakes you've been making for twenty years." Another time, McGraw benched Terry when the first baseman was three minutes late for curfew because a movie ran long. Late in the following day's game, when a teammate relayed the message that McGraw wanted him to pinch-hit, Terry slowly sauntered to the space directly in front of the manager, and slowly put on his shoes. Then he stepped up to the plate and hit a home run that won the game.

In 1924, Terry would be sharing first base chores with George "High Pockets" Kelly, because McGraw wanted to add Terry's left-handed power to the batting lineup. Kelly had joined the Giants in 1920, and after a slow start—he was 0–19 before getting his first hit, a triple against the St. Louis Cardinals—

Kelly was soon drawing comparisons to Babe Ruth. In 1921 he led the National League with twenty-three home runs. During one game in September 1923, Kelly hit a single, a double and three home runs.

Kelly and Terry were just two elements in a powerful lineup that was coming off a pennant championship. At shortstop was Travis Jackson, a .300 hitter and future Hall of Famer. Third base was manned by an inexperienced rookie, Freddie Lindstrom, who had replaced the injured Heinie Groh. The pitching rotation was solid if not overwhelming: Art Nehf (14–4 in 1924), Jack Bentley (16–5), "Handsome Hugh" McQuillan (14–8), and Virgil Barnes (16–10). Catching them was veteran catcher Hank Gowdy, a solid if unspectacular player.

Most commentators predicted easy pennants for the Giants in the National League and for the Yankees in the American League, although some thought the Yankees might have trouble winning the American League crown against the hard-hitting Cleveland Indians. Denman Thompson of the *Washington Star* put the Yankees and Indians first and second; after that would come "a scramble between the Tigers, Nationals, Athletics and Browns, with the two hosiery outfits—Red and White—for what's left."

Baseball magazine had Washington finishing seventh. Others weren't so sure. The Associated Press wrote, "The 1924 race, baseball players say, promises to be another record season from the standpoint of attendance and close finishes." A few sportswriters even showed some enthusiasm for Washington. A writer for the *Washington Star* exclaimed that in preseason games Joe Judge was "showing midseason form," a phrase echoed in a report about Walter Johnson as well: "The war-scarred veteran of 17 campaigns and holder of several major league records, is displaying midseason form and has given Griffith's club an air of confidence."

Manager Bucky Harris had been inspired during training camp, drilling his players in the fundamentals and preaching the importance of hustle. But one player was having trouble getting with the Harris program. Goose Goslin had shown up at camp out of shape and lacking enthusiasm. When he failed to run out a ball he had grounded back to the pitcher, Harris had a sit-down talk with the outfielder, encouraging him to "put more punch" in his training. Finally, on April 7, Harris sent Goose back to Washington with strict orders to get back in shape. "I would be ashamed to start in a league a man so unfit for duty," Harris said. "Goose is overweight and certainly has not strengthened his legs sufficiently to withstand the strain of play in the field."

Babe Ruth was also often unable to play that spring, but for a different reason. An April 6 exhibition game between the Yankees and the Memphis Robins in Nashville had to be called off in the ninth inning with the score tied 8–8. A "ring of small boys," reported one paper, surrounded Babe Ruth in right field whenever he tried to catch a fly ball. Ruth changed to first base, but the crowd around him only got bigger. When the Yankees went to bat in the first half of the tenth inning, the admiring throngs had grown so immense that the game had to be called. "The contagion of hero worship," reported one paper, "infected 10,000 people."

⚾

IT WAS OPENING DAY AGAIN, April 15, 1924, a beautiful sunny afternoon in Washington, and a record crowd of 17,581 turned out to Griffith Stadium to enjoy the action as the Senators began their season with a game against the Philadelphia Athletics. With the U.S. Marines marching band providing musical accompaniment, President Calvin Coolidge threw out the first ball.

According to the papers, the country was still reeling under the weight of the carnage of the First World War, the Teapot Dome affair, and the Black Sox scandal. But on Opening Day the dark events all seemed to fade away: "Baseball drove politics and Teapot Dome into the background, temporarily at least, today when 'what did Babe Ruth do today?' became the most important question of the nation," wrote the Associated Press.

Attendance at the park had gone from 234,000 in 1919 to 359,000 in 1920, then over 450,000 in 1921 and 1922. Fans loved the improvements in the park, which had now officially been rechristened Griffith Stadium, though at least one fan questioned the competence of Griffith's handymen: the roof of the new bleacher was oddly higher than that of the old, prompting Shirley Povich to comment that it looked as if "the carpenter had worked with a bottle, not a hammer."

The Senators did not disappoint, beating Philadelphia 4–0. It was Walter Johnson's 102nd shutout; his strikeouts now totaled 3,074. Joe Judge started his season with a triple down the left-field line and was then driven home by Sam Rice. Judge was also, according to the *Washington Star,* "responsible for the best bit of fielding of the fray." Athletics left fielder Curly Simmons had grounded to Peckinpaugh at short. Peck then threw wildly, "but Joe leapt high to spear the ball, then touched the runner as he went by to save the veteran shortstop from an error." Judge was also part of a pickoff when Muddy Ruel fired a bullet to him from behind the plate.

When the Yankees came to Washington for a four-day series on April 19, the *Washington Star* called them "that aggregation of diamond prima donnas." Ruth didn't even finish the first game. In the fifth inning, after being called out on strikes, he disgustedly tossed his bat in the air and umpire Billy Evans ejected him from the game. Joe Judge led off the fourth with a triple, making the first of Washington's twelve hits. The Senators won, then followed up with a 12–3 victory in the second game, only to lose games three and four. The Yankees returned home and raised the American League pennant over Yankee Stadium in celebration of their 1923 season. In the National League, the Giants were already on top with a record of 5–1.

The Senators began to slide. On April 26 they went down to the Athletics 2–1, and found themselves at 4–7. The team batting average was .257 and they had made eighteen errors. On April 29 they were drubbed by the Red Sox, 15–3.

Then they headed to New York for a rematch with the Yankees, and the dismaying slump was checked. On May 1 they beat their powerful opponents 3–2, employing the classic Washington formula: get behind great pitching, provide great defense, and play old-style offense, getting men on base and driving them home with solid base hits. Washington had a 3–0 lead going into the seventh inning when Johnson, who up to that point had allowed only two hits, gave up consecutive triples. Marberry entered the game with a 3–1 lead, one out and a man on third. Yankees catcher Wally Schang grounded out, scoring the man on third. The next two batters got on base with a single and a bunt. Marberry intentionally walked Ruth, then forced the next batter to pop out.

The game was a harbinger of the Senators' season. They would often find themselves in a close game but through brilliant fielding or just plain determination pull out a victory. "Everyone gives Harris credit for [the team's fighting spirit]," Frank Young wrote in the *Washington Post,* "never beaten until the game is over."

"Never beaten"—this would be the team's motto for the rest of this extraordinary year.

A vivid example of Washington's fearlessness occurred in another face-off with the Yankees (a story often told by Al Schacht). Before the game, Yankees pitcher Bob Shawkey boasted to the Senators that he was going to knock down every player in the lineup, and then proceeded to do so. In the third inning Harris, itching for revenge, bunted down the first-base line, hoping that Shawkey would cover first. Shawkey didn't, so Bucky stole second, bulldozing over the shortstop Everett Scott, then moving to third on a wild throw and eventually scoring. After the inning, Babe Ruth came up to Harris. "Little man, he said, "if I get off first base, watch out." Harris told the Senators pitcher to "pass the monkey" when Ruth came up. Ruth tried to steal, although his only intention was payback on Harris at second base, and Bucky hockey-checked the Bambino so fiercely that, according to Schacht, "Ruth tumbled halfway out to centerfield." Harris held the ball and glared at Ruth, growling, "Keep coming, monkey, and you'll get the ball right between the eyes."

For much of the summer, the Senators were never far from first place, usually separated by just a few games from New York and Detroit. Nobody had expected this, but after a brief May slump in which they hit the bottom of the standings, the Senators caught fire. "Washington got hotter quicker than any team I ever saw," Babe Ruth would later say. Bucky Harris, the young man once derisively dismissed as Griffith's Folly, was increasingly recognized as a key motivator: the team wanted to win for a manager they held in high regard.

The Senators stayed in the race by making vital replacements of players at the right time. When outfielder Nemo Leibold went into a slump in June, Griffith quickly replaced him with a "peppery outfielder" named Wid Mathews, noted for his irascibility. Mathews had initially gone into the majors after batting .332 on the Milwaukee team of the minor league American Association. Drafted by Connie Mack's Philadelphia A's, he arrived at training camp in Montgomery, Alabama, in 1923 and made an announcement: "I'm not looking for any utility job." Mathews wanted to play full-time.

Mack made Mathews one of the regular squad, and the young player responded brilliantly. However, towards the end of the season he had an altercation with Mack. Mathews had made a mistake while on base, Mack scolded him and Mathews talked back. Mack sent Mathews back to Milwaukee and the minor leagues; angry Philadelphia fans insisted that he had been railroaded.

Mathews's troubles continued in Milwaukee. In May 1924 he got into an argument with Brewers president Otto Brohert, calling him "a cheap stiff." He went back home to Metropolis, Illinois, to sulk in his tent. Griffith snapped him up.

When Mathews arrived in their outfield, the Senators were in the middle of a winning streak. On June 4 the team had won five of their last seven games. Rice was batting .335, Judge .334, Goslin .324 and Ossie Bluege .310, the same as Muddy Ruel. Boston, New York and Detroit were on top in the American League, but the Senators were just under .500 and in fourth place.

In his first game back in the majors, Wid Mathews went two for four, a single and a triple. He also drove in a run and made spectacular plays in the field. Griffith's shrewd judgment of talent was once again vindicated.

⚾

BASEBALL WAS A MUCH MORE active and physical game in the 1920s than it would become after midcentury, and injuries were hard to avoid. Granddad had broken his leg back in 1917, and his ordeals during the 1924 season show what kind of day-to-day perils players faced. On May 28, Babe Ruth drove a shot that smacked him right above his knee. On June 7, a ball thrown from the short outfield struck him on the jaw, making it difficult for him to move his head because of neck pain. He came back quickly, but then on June 10 he reinjured the leg Ruth had hit. He was sent back to Washington for x-rays. "It is unfortunate that Judge is forced out of action," John Keller wrote in the *Washington Star,* "for he has been playing the game of his career this season. Joe's hitting has been hard and timely and his fielding of a spectacular character." And he praised Judge for initiating double plays, a category in which he led.

Judge wouldn't be back at first base until June 22, but Harris had another strong player to fill in for him. Replacement "Mule" Shirley drove in four runs in the Senators' 12–1 victory over St. Louis. Shirley was one of many first basemen who would threaten Joe's job over the years, although he fought them all off successfully until he was felled by appendicitis in 1931. Griffith promoted rivals because he thought that Joe played best when he felt under pressure to keep his job. "I have to pay two first basemen to get the most out of Judge," the Old Fox once said.

Even without Judge, the team continued to play strongly. On June 20, Fred Marberry saved a 3–2 lead in the twelfth inning against the Athletics; by this time he had won seven out of eight games. On June 22 they beat the Athletics 5–4 before a capacity crowd at Griffith Stadium. The fans were entertained by Al Schacht and his comedy partner Nick Altrock. At this point, Schacht had largely abandoned any hope of reviving his pitching career and was concentrating his energies on comedy. In one routine, Altrock stood at first, pretending to be drunk while Schacht, at third, tossed a rubber ball that bounced off Altrock's head. And they did a skit on a famous burlesque dancer, using a string of hot dogs in place of the snake she employed. Another of their classics was a send-up they had first unveiled during the 1922 World Series—a bullfighting scene spoofing the steamy Rudolph Valentino movie *Blood and Sand,* in which a goat was used as the bull and Altrock in drag as the love interest to Schacht's matador.

The crowd also liked Wid Mathews, playing in his first game in front of a Washington crowd. Mathews was anxious— so much so that he tried to get in on every play. When a ball was driven near the grandstand in left field and caught by Goslin, Mathews, the center fielder, was no more than ten feet away.

On June 23 the Senators were in New York for another four-game series with the Yankees. Washington was in fourth place, but so few games separated them from leaders Boston and New York that a sweep of the series could put them in first place. The Yankees had beaten Washington sixteen out of twenty-two games in 1923, and the Senators knew that the road to the pennant went through Ruth and the Yankees.

The Senators began by winning both games of a double-header, 5–3 and 4–2. In the first game, George Mogridge held New York to nine hits, and Tom Zachary allowed only eight in the second. The next day, the Senators prevailed again, 4–3. The lead would have been greater had not Judge been "robbed of at least a triple" by a tour de force of fielding in the ninth inning, according to an article the following day; to make the difficult catch, Babe Ruth made a dramatic dash to the right-field bleacher screen.

Washington, now 32–26, was suddenly in first place. The team had won their last eight games, and eleven of their last thirteen. The Yankees were 30–26 and Detroit was 34–30. The Senators were playing, as the *Washington Star* put it, with "all the enthusiasm one would expect to find in some big college athletic team."

The Griffmen then beat the Yankees for a fourth straight time, 3–2. Then on June 26, in front of 35,000 back home at Griffith, Walter Johnson pitched his 105th career shutout, blanking the Athletics 5–0. Three of the Senators' runs came off the bat of Joe Judge.

Washington fans were beginning to suspect that this was not a typical Senators team that would fade in the long summer of a hard season. An extended headline in an anonymous story in the *Washington Star* on June 27, 1924, captured the spirit of the city:

FAN OF YEARS AGO, SICK OF GAME,
BALL PARK ROOTER ONCE MORE;
REVIVAL OF LONG CHERISHED PENNANT
HOPES BRINGS CYNICAL GROUCHES
TO CHEER THE NATIONALS

The article related the saga of a certain unnamed fan:

> [His] confidence in his home team as a pennant contender
> had gradually withered and dried during long years of dia-
> mond fiascoes. . . . [The fan had] made a vow to himself that
> he was through with the game forever. This temperamental,
> and perhaps, un-sportsmanlike man swore that he never again
> would enter the portals of American League Park until the
> Washington team was in first place.

Yet something had changed:

> Yesterday this same fan, somewhat the worse for wear and
> showing the effects of his seven-year itch to see a ball game,
> swept out of his office at 1 o'clock and turned his steering
> wheel out Georgia Avenue Way. . . . When the first game had
> ended, 5 to 0 in favor of Washington, a fan leapt into the field,
> closely followed by thousands of his ilk. It was the grouch.
> He felt seven years younger as he pushed and crushed his way
> toward the Washington dugout in enthusiasm over the victory.

It was around this time that the Senators picked up another
important player, pitcher Warren "Curly" Ogden. Put on waivers
by the Athletics, Ogden had a dreadful career record of 2–9,
with a 1924 tally up to this point of 0–3 and a startling ERA of
almost six runs. But whatever the Old Fox saw in the 23-year-
old right-hander bloomed when he got to Washington. He went
from being a reliever to a starting pitcher, and would win eight
straight games towards the end of the season, including three
shutouts.

On July 4, twenty thousand fans turned out to Griffith Stadium to watch the first of five games against the Yankees. The
team was hot, and the *Star* noted the large number of women
in attendance:

Even since the Griffmen returned home a week ago leading the league, one of the outstanding features of the gallery that had followed them has been the increasing numbers of women. [That Independence Day] the bright colors of the attractive feminine costumes flashed their scarlet, lavender and yellow in the mellow sunshine, a relieving contrast to the conventional garb of their male escorts.

It was known that Walter Johnson had female admirers, as did Joe Judge. In a profile that ran later in the season, the *Star* put it this way:

Judge generally is accounted one of the niftiest first sackers in the business today and is recognized as rivaling Tawny, Chase and Sisler [other premier first basemen in the game] for the ease with which he handles all manner of chances around his station. He is the poetry of motion on a ball field, and for this reason attracts admiration of fair fans as well as their escorts, but his worth is not confined to fielding. Few pitchers relish the sight of Judge coming up to bat.

For my bashful grandfather and his family, his new fame was often unsettling. Before she died in 2002, his daughter and my aunt Anita remembered being at a game in the early 1920s when Joe belted an extra-base hit. A woman sitting behind her became so excited that she grabbed Anita and began to shake her, shouting "That's your daddy!" Almost eighty years later, my aunt still felt slightly miffed by the fan's fervor. "It hurt!" she groused.

Such embarrassments are of course one of the costs of stardom; but as Joe's grandson, brought up in the city where he was admired, I was lucky enough to experience the benefits, as well as the occasional slight inconveniences, of his renown. Decades later, there were still small pockets in Washington where Joe Judge was a name to conjure with. Growing up, I would sometimes be asked, usually by an old-timer, if I was related to him; sure enough, when I said yes I would likely be treated to protracted rhapsodies about Joe Judge and the old Washington Senators. In the 1980s, while I was in college, I got a job working in a bar, and when the owner's father found out I was related to Joe Judge, he practically swooned. From that moment on I could do no wrong; no matter how many times I showed up late or how many orders I blew, I could never manage to get myself fired.

Women and teenage girls were attracted to my grandfather in ways that sometimes made him squirm. One story I haven't been able to nail down with any certainty involves a woman who called the house claiming that she had had an affair with him and was carrying his baby. Everyone acquainted with Joe Judge knew the charge was ridiculous—Goslin, maybe, but never Judge. The only time the story ever came up was when Alma Judge was telling my mother about how hard it was at times being married to a famous man. She mentioned this incident of the woman calling with her accusations, adding that she was crazy and that ballplayers were subjected to that kind of thing all the time.

The presence of female fans didn't help the Senators in their series against the Yankees. They lost three games out of four. The main attraction, of course, was the Babe. The circulation manager of the *Washington Star* had taken six hundred paperboys to the first game. During batting practice, Nick Altrock sent one into the left-field bleacher, where the boys were sitting: there was "a mad scramble for the pill." And when Ruth signed a ball and hurled it into the same section, bedlam ensued.

Washington fans were using a new tactic, very loud whistling, to distract opposing teams, but it didn't work on the Yankees. Neither team was ready to accept defeat. The symbolic image of their determination was provided on that occasion when Ruth, chasing a foul ball hit by Judge, was knocked cold after he ran slap into the right-field wall. In a photo of the incident, reprinted in several baseball books, Ruth looks quite dead: he's on his back, eyes closed, mouth agape. Yet he quickly recovered and returned to the game. These were teams that simply would not die.

One of the main reasons the Senators stayed in the race that summer was not only the return to form by Johnson and the strong play by veterans Peckinpaugh, Rice and Judge, but the hitting of Goose Goslin. His enthusiasm for baseball renewed—he had evidently taken Bucky Harris's preseason counseling to heart—Goose had managed to raise his batting average from .277 on May 15 to .310 by the beginning of July. By the end of July he was the fourth-best hitter in the American League.

But hitting continued to get better all over the league. On July 26, two headlines told the story: larger-than-life Babe Ruth was leading the league in batting, while at age thirty-seven, Ty Cobb, symbol of the driving, slap-hitting, base-stealing past, announced he was thinking of retirement. Cobb said his one regret was that he hadn't done any good for humanity. "If I had my time over again I would probably be a surgeon instead of a ballplayer," he said, adding, "Everyone will have forgotten me in ten years." Like most athletes—including Joe Judge—Cobb had trouble letting go. His last year would actually be 1928.

After going 18–14–1 during a long at-home stand, by the end of July the Senators were still in a dead heat with New York and Detroit and headed out to play western teams, including the Cleveland Indians. Playing exhibition games with minor league teams was a common practice then, but when Griffith was asked if the team planned on playing any on this road trip, he said, "I beg to state that manager Harris does not feel as though he should book any games at present. As we figure on being in the pennant race all the way, and he needs to preserve the strength of his club in every way possible."

The Senators' tour through the West (or what was considered the West back then) was a disaster. They lost six games in a row—five of them to the fourth-place St. Louis Browns—and soon found themselves close to dropping out of the hunt. The midsummer heat in St. Louis, unbearable even to a team from the District of Columbia, may have had something to do with the losses. Third baseman Ossie Bluege recalled:

> [The St. Louis field] was as hard as concrete and it felt like running on hot coals. The ground crew would water it down after practice. There was so much steam rising it hit you in the face. I saw a number of guys faint standing in the infield.

And Bluege described how at night,

the air in the hotel room was sweltering. You couldn't get a fan. You'd douse yourself in water and try to get some sleep. The next day you'd go to the ballpark feeling like a wrung-out dishrag.

Once again, Harris made adjustments and the team fought back. While Wid Mathews had been invaluable in the beginning of the season, his play had since become erratic. (Mathews had led the league in errors as a rookie with the A's in 1923.) Teams had adjusted to Mathews's hitting style. He was left-handed and tended to pull his hits into right field, so opposing teams started moving the outfield over to close the gap, and his average dropped. In a move that outraged Washington fans, Griffith traded Mathews and two other players so that he could purchase a new center fielder, Earl McNeely, from the Sacramento team in the Pacific Coast League.

Griffith hadn't even seen McNeely play, going on the word of scout Joe Engel. Sacramento wanted $75,000 for McNeely, but Griffith talked them down to $35,000. McNeely joined the team in Chicago, and when Griffith offered his hand, joking that he finally got to meet the man he had paid so much money for, McNeely didn't offer his hand back; he had injured his arm the previous week and couldn't lift it above his hip. Griffith called Commissioner Landis, demanding that the deal be scrapped. Landis said no, and the results were a mixed blessing. McNeely would hit well for the remainder of the regular season, but his play in one game of the World Series would make the Senators desperately miss Mathews's strong arm.

Washington won only four of the thirteen games played on their western tour. Against the Indians, Tigers and Browns, Goslin hit .213, Judge .266 and Leibold .220. Only Sam Rice hit over .300 during the trip. On August 10, the day before returning home, the Senators were in third place, behind Detroit and the first-place Yankees.

But back at home base, the team came to life once again. Johnson pitched his 106th career shutout on August 12. On August 16, the Tigers, one-and-a-half games ahead of the Senators, came to Washington for a five-game series. Detroit won the first game 5–2, behind the strong pitching of Earl Whithill and the play of Ty Cobb. In his twentieth season, Cobb went 2–4, including a triple. The next day the Senators came out on top, 8–1. They beat the Tigers in the next two games, 4–3 and 5–3.

For the rest of August, the Senators and the Yankees stayed neck and neck, with the Tigers in the race until the end of the month. On August 25, while the Yankees were beating Cleveland 8–3, Walter Johnson threw his 107th shutout in St. Louis. It was the Senators' eighth win in a row, and they enjoyed parity with the Yankees until Ruth hit a game-winning home run later in the day against Cleveland.

A half-game away from the Yankees, the Senators again went to New York for a four-game series. They won the first game 11–6, filling the bases four times in one inning and playing spectacular defense; and they took the second game 5–1, but got a scare in the eighth inning when Yankee Wally Schang, batting against Johnson, walloped a ball back to the mound, striking the pitcher's right hand. After making the throw to first, Walter sank to the ground in agony. He was surrounded by players from both teams, and after a few minutes he tried to pitch again but found he could not. Fred Marberry was called in for relief.

Johnson was sent back to Washington for x-rays, but the injury would turn out not to be serious, much to the despair of other teams—or so people joked. The *New York Herald Tribune* made this observation when Johnson went down:

> Yankee players, as well as Washington athletes, gathered around the stricken pitcher on the greensward. It is supposed that the Senators were offering him sympathy. It is also deemed that [Yankees manager] Miller Huggins tried to persuade Johnson that the only way to treat a bruised thumb is to break it off.

The *New York Times* had this to say:

> They [the Senators] looked more like a championship club than any other outfit that has yet appeared at the stadium. If the general opposition isn't any stronger than that offered by the Yanks the Capital Club will waltz through to its first American League Pennant.

It wouldn't exactly be a waltz. The Senators lost the third game, a pitching duel between Curly Ogden and the Yankees' Waite Hoyt, 2–1. Still and all, the Senators had hit their stride. On August 31, Bucky Harris said,

> I honestly believe I have the hardest working ball club in the league right now. That does not mean that other clubs aren't giving everything they have to the pennant fight. But I have not yet seen any team that can match the one I am in charge of for gaminess.

Goslin and Rice in particular seemed driven. In the first two games against the Yankees, Rice went six for ten with three of the hits going for extra bases, and Goslin hit two homers, a triple, a double and three singles in nine trips to the plate.

The Senators won the fourth game in New York, and were in first place when they were greeted by thousands of fans upon returning home to Union Station. Washington was rapidly developing pennant fever. On September 1, over twenty thousand people came to Griffith Stadium to watch the Senators beat the Athletics 5–3. Joe Judge hit a triple, two doubles and a single in four trips to the plate. Fans had come in large groups from the Navy Yard, Bloomingdale's department stores, the boards of trade and commerce, and the Manufacturers Association. The female fans rang klaxons and cowbells, and the crowd cheered wildly for Goose Goslin even as he took batting practice.

On September 5, the Senators were invited to the White House by their greatest fan, Calvin Coolidge. Joe Judge, because of yet another leg injury he had sustained playing against Boston, arrived using a cane. Coolidge was still grieving over the death of his son by blood poisoning two months earlier, but he told the team that he would love to be able to attend the World Series in Washington and root for them.

Washington had an overall two-game lead when they went to Philadelphia to start the last three weeks of the season. Johnson downed the Athletics on September 8 for his twentieth victory of the year. The Senators took three out of four of the games, then moved on to Detroit to face Ty Cobb's Tigers. Cobb, now thirty-seven, had played in every Tigers game, going to the plate

◀ Father and son—Joseph Patrick Judge and Joseph Ignatius Judge, 1918

▼ Alma Gauvreau Judge, age 89, in 1979

▲ Judge farm, County Mayo, Ireland

▲ 1909 Senators, one of the worst teams in baseball history (56 games behind Detroit). Walter Johnson is the last man on the right.

▲ Al Schacht and Nick Altrock do their comedy routine during the 1924 World Series.

▲ Bucky Harris and John McGraw, rival
field generals in the 1924 World Series

▲ Muddy Ruel and Walter Johnson, the
Senators' battery

▲ Griffith Stadium, the place to be in Washington in the 1920s

▲ Goose Goslin, lifetime .316 hitter and Hall of Famer

▲ Sam Rice, lifetime .322 hitter and Hall of Famer

▲ Walter Johnson and Ty Cobb—the nicest man in baseball and the nastiest

▲ Clark Griffith—player, manager, owner

▲ Out or safe? Joe Judge and Freddie Lindstrom in Game One

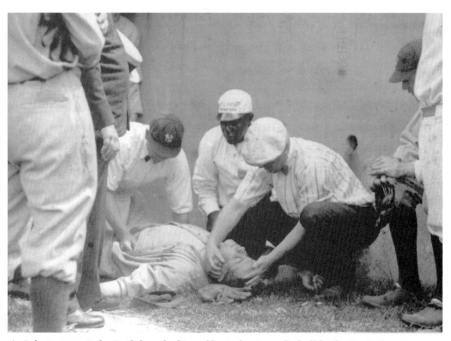

▲ July 5, 1924. Babe Ruth knocks himself out chasing a fly ball hit by Joe Judge at Griffith Stadium.

Joe Judge—the perfect swing ▶

▲ With Walter Johnson on Joe Judge Day, June 28, 1930

◀ Coaching with my dad at Georgetown University

▲ Serving breakfast at Joe Judge's Restaurant

▲ Celebration dinner for the Washington Senators, October 1, 1924

625 times. Johnson won a game for Washington on September 13, but then the Senators dropped the last two. The letdown was somewhat compensated for when word came in that Walter Johnson had been named the American League Most Valuable Player for 1924. "I never dreamed of such a thing," Johnson said with his unaffected modesty. He had received fifty-five votes out of a possible sixty-four from baseball writers.

Still, this honor could not mean as much to Johnson as a pennant would, and the Detroit games were ones Washington couldn't afford to lose. Even if the Tigers had by now been mathematically eliminated, the Yankees were not about to give up. They had stayed close, and while the Senators were being mauled by the Tigers, the Yankees were sweeping Chicago. The two teams were now deadlocked, 82–59.

The enthusiasm among Washingtonians was now coming to a boil. Some argued that the fans' mania would actually compromise the team's chances. The *Washington Post* ran a letter from one Harry Kabat, who announced he was founding the "Save Your Lid Club." The writer complained that the fans' customary showering of the field with straw hats after a great play was a bad idea. He cited one game where Earl McNeely hit a triple in the eighth with the score close and rain approaching. Rather than let the teams finish the game before the storm, "the untimely barrage of straw hats marred the rally and delayed the game to such an extent" that, had it rained sooner, the Senators could not have come back to win the game. "Even if the fans cannot actually help a team win," wrote Kabat testily, "I do know they can help a team lose." Whatever the ins and outs of this pivotal debate, the Old Fox showed his confidence in the team by announcing he was adding seats to Griffith Stadium, expanding its capacity to 36,000.

For the next two weeks, and indeed until the last weekend of the season, the Yankees and the Senators were in a dead heat. The Senators beat Boston two out of three games, losing the third game 6–2 before thirty thousand people, up to that point the largest crowd ever at Griffith Stadium. Fans were now being turned away from the box office. At the *Washington Post* building downtown a giant magnetic scoreboard was erected with a facsimile field. Thousands gathered around the sign during the games as the season approached its thrilling climax.

By this time almost everybody in the country, not just Washingtonians, was rooting for the underdog Senators. This groundswell of sympathy had been evident as early as August. On the 28th of that month, the Senators were in New York for the last series of the year against the Yankees. They were down 6–3 in the eighth when they staged a rally, scoring eight runs in one inning and winning the game 11–6. A reporter described the scene:

> That eighth inning explosion caused one of the wildest demonstrations ever seen anywhere. The big crowd stood and roared and howled encouragement as the fighting Griffs drove one pitcher after another from the rubber. A shower of straw hats followed every resounding wallop, the Washington dugout was bedlam, exuding dancing athletes, old gloves, towels, caps and shoes, and accompanied, as on a grand organ, by the roaring of some 25,000 fans.

The columnist Damon Runyon wrote:

> It will be a great thing for baseball if Washington goes into the World Series. This is treasonable from a New Yorker, but true. New York has become satiated, blasé, with baseball championships. It no longer appreciates the thrill of the World Series. The country at large cannot work up much interest when two New York clubs are fighting for the championship of the baseball world. It was novel, thrilling for a couple of years to see the teams of the greater city struggle for supremacy; then it became monotonous.

Even Yankees manager Miller Huggins faced the truth. "I've told my players and talked over with them the fact that everyone is against us," he said on September 10. "Even the fans down in New York seem to take a certain delight in seeing some of us beaten."

⌒

ONE REASON THAT THE SENATORS had become a national cause was Walter Johnson. He had poured his genius into so many losing Washington teams that the world was ready to see him finally win one. Johnson was admired for his character, so at odds with the pugnacity of Cobb and the vulgarity of Ruth. The Big Train seemed a throwback to a simpler, quieter, more decent America. He never raised his voice or scolded teammates who had made a mistake. In fact he would comfort them, even if the mistake had cost the Senators a game. The only time anyone remembered Johnson ever losing his temper was when he saw a policeman trying to remove a black boy who used to hang around the park doing odd jobs to get close to the players. Johnson erupted, going so far as to say "Dadgum ya!" to the cop.

The night after beating the Yankees on August 29, Johnson, Harris and other teammates attended a Ziegfeld Follies show on Broadway as the guests of Will Rogers. Rogers had dedicated his September 28 *New York Times* column to the Senators' pitcher. It summed up the sentiments of many in the country:

> [Johnson] is still just a country boy, yet as I am writing this there is more real genuine interest in him than there is in a presidential election. Who is the fellow that he can do this? How is it that one single individual can have the sincere good wishes of the President of the United States, the Congress, the Senate, the Judges of our Supreme Court, even the sincere good wishes of the other two presidential candidates? (I suppose this is the only time in political history that three candidates ever agreed heartily on one thing.) He is not slick, yet there are lots and lots of people in all parts of our country that never saw him or hope to see him, that are actually [pulling] for fate to smile on this big old country boy. . . .
>
> I don't suppose that ever in the history of any sporting event has sentiment played so big a part as it is playing in the case of this one man this year. [Christy] Mathewson, the great pitcher, was the idol of millions of well-wishers, but he was on a winning team. He was in the limelight all the time, but here is a man, Johnson, that has been with a team at the bottom of the list so long that the only way he could get any satisfaction out of a newspaper was to stand on his head. He never grumbled, he could have sulked, and demanded and been traded to any other team in the league and been with a

pennant winner almost every year and made lots of money. Lots of them have been doing it and they are playing today and all has been forgotten. But not with this old country boy. That is why he stands in public estimation today where he does. Had he deserted Washington he could have just been known as a wonderful pitcher, perhaps losing fewer games with a good team than any pitcher the game ever knew. But as it is, he is known as a wonderful man, and today the entire baseball world is not pulling for Johnson the pitcher; they are pulling for Johnson the man.

Johnson was aware of the stakes. "I always hoped that I would get a chance in the World Series before my career on the diamond has ended," he said, "and if this dream comes true, 1924 will be the year [against which] everything else will be measured."

☁

AS THE SEASON APPROACHED ITS end, Bucky Harris was trying to get any advantage he could. He acquired a player who would play a small but crucial part in Senators history, Wade Lefler. He had hit .369 in the Eastern League, and had a fielding average of .978 in the outfield and .981 at his other position, first base. Lefler was no doubt recruited as security for first base and strength at the plate, but perhaps Griffith also wanted extra pressure on Judge to perform down the stretch. "Due to the susceptibility of Joe Judge to injury," the *Washington Post* reported, "and the weakness of Mule Shirley at the plate, it is possible that Lefler will be stationed at first base before the season is over." That would never happen, but Lefler would play a pivotal part at the end of the regular season, only to disappear afterwards into obscurity.

On September 17, the Senators downed the Indians 3–2. It was Johnson's twelfth straight win. The Senators had played twenty games over .500 for the last month of the season, and even as they continued trading first place with the Yankees, Griffith was planning to host the World Series. In a meeting with Commissioner Landis on September 17, he announced that the new outfield bleachers would bring the capacity to 32,245— larger than any other park except Yankee Stadium.

As if the Senators needed more pressure, on September 21 Commissioner Landis announced that the World Series would begin in Washington on October 4. Landis had met with representatives of the five best teams in baseball, and it was decided that the first, second and sixth games would be played in the American League city, and the third, fourth and fifth in the National League city. If a seventh game was necessary, the location would be decided by a coin toss. In his announcement, Landis blurted out that the first game would be played in Washington. It was not recorded whether anyone corrected his slip of the tongue.

Indeed, the District of Columbia began to prepare a ceremonial tribute to the team. On September 25, the papers announced that President and Mrs. Coolidge would preside over a parade down Pennsylvania Avenue for the Senators when they returned at the end of the month from their latest road trip. The procession would wind up at the Ellipse, which was being set up with loudspeakers for the occasion. Melvin C. Hazen, chairman of the welcoming committee, asked the businesses along Pennsylvania Avenue to put out fliers. He also planned an "automobile parade, in which every follower of the Nats who possesses an automobile is invited to take part." After the parade, the players, politicians and luminaries would have dinner at the Occidental Hotel.

There was only one problem: the Senators had not yet clinched the pennant. By September 25, their lead over the Yankees was two games with four games left to go. While the Yankees were in Philadelphia, the Senators would play a final four-game series in Boston. Walter Johnson had not done well against the Red Sox all season long, losing twice and being driven out of the game early another two times. Nevertheless, Johnson had a thirteen-game winning streak going into the first game. And Sam Rice had gotten hits in thirty-one straight games, a baseball record that would stand until 1933, when it was beaten by Heinie Manush.

Both Johnson and Rice had their streaks broken the following day, the Senators losing to Boston 2–1, despite the fact that, as in New York, Cleveland and elsewhere, Red Sox fans were openly rooting for Washington. In the seventh inning, Johnson had to leave the game with a numb arm after a line drive had whacked him on the elbow. Meanwhile, in Philadelphia, the Yankees crushed the Athletics 7–0.

The Senators' lead was down to one game.

That evening, the *Washington Star* groaned that the players seemed flaccid during their losing effort and showed no "snap." Perhaps the long, grueling season had finally taken its toll and the Senators were out of gas. The mood at their hotel was anxious and dour; there was none of the usual humorous kidding among the players. Faces were shrouded with doubt. Earl McNeely had played poorly in the game, and frankly described his feelings that night:

> You know, it was the first time I realized just what our pennant chances actually [were]. Before the game today I began thinking about the World Series and how wonderful it would be. And the whole thing scared me.

Walter Johnson recalled that "everybody, from Clark Griffith on down, was in a pretty nervous state of mind, to say the least." Some of the players were so nervous they spent the night walking up and down the street or sitting in front of the hotel.

I have never been able to find out if my grandfather was one of these players, but I often imagine him in his Irish cap and suit, pacing outside the Boston hotel, staring anxiously into the middle distance. To make matters even worse for him, the next day was Sunday, and the blue laws in Boston forbade games on the Sabbath. He and his teammates had another twenty-four hours to worry over their fate.

The game began ominously when the Senators' starter George Mogridge was tagged for four runs in the first inning. Harris immediately replaced him with Fred Marberry, who shut down the Red Sox offensive. In the fifth inning, Goslin singled and was followed by Judge, who bunted and safely reached first. Muddy Ruel followed and was hit by a pitch. With the bases loaded, Wade Lefler was sent in to pinch-hit for Marberry. He slapped a line drive to deep right, bringing in all three runners. Lefler tried to stretch the hit into a triple and was thrown out at third, but the score was 5–4. The Senators then scored two more runs in the sixth to win the game. The Boston crowd, which had booed Boston pitcher Howard Eamke when he struck out Roger Peckinpaugh, went crazy. (Wade Lefler would play only six games in his entire career, all of them for the Senators at the end of the 1924 season. He went five for eight for Washington, retiring from baseball with a .556 lifetime average.)

Suddenly, news came in from Philadelphia. The Athletics had beaten the Yankees 4–3. The Senators were up two games, with two games left. The worst they could do was tie.

The news electrified the Senators—they were actually within reach of their first pennant. The next day, as the Yankees were losing, they downed Boston 4–2, preventing the Red Sox from scoring twice when the bases were loaded. The game ended on a double play, and when Harris's throw snapped into Judge's glove at first base, the team went wild. Their dugout erupted, the players tossing bats and gloves onto the field, which was already covered with straw hats. Clark Griffith could barely make it out of the stadium for all the well-wishers.

When the last out was made, Walter Johnson had been warming up in the bullpen in case he was needed. A witness described the scene:

> As the great Walter neared the stand, 15,000 folks rose up and gave him a cheer that came right out of the heart of a nation. A few ran out to shake his hand; others slapped him on the back; but Walter didn't hurry; neither did he look up in response to the noisy ovation. He kept his head down because there were tears in his eyes.

The Washington, D.C., commissioner issued a formal proclamation congratulating the team. Grace Coolidge brought the news to her husband, Calvin, who sent a telegram to Bucky Harris:

> Heartiest congratulations to you and your team for your great work in bringing Washington its first pennant. We of Washington are proud of you and behind you all the way to the world's championship!

When the news of the Senators' victory flashed over the downtown scoreboard in Washington at 4:42, cheering and shouting erupted and traffic cops forgot the traffic. "This dignified old capital of the United States has gone baseball mad," the *Washington Star* reported, noting that the city's usual business had gone "straight to pot." Supreme Court justice William McKenna allowed as how he felt a "distinct thrill." And even the cloistered monks at the Franciscan monastery in the quiet Washington neighborhood of Brookland—which to this day is still home to Catholic University and the religious orders—felt the excitement. After the last out came in over the radio, one monk was seen slapping another on the back.

Already, ten thousand fans were congregating at Griffith Stadium to try and get tickets for the first World Series game against the Giants, who had withstood a late-season push by the Dodgers to retain the National League championship. One man, a wounded World War I veteran, was crushed by the crowd; he collapsed and was sent home in a cab. (He would later be given a ticket by a compassionate fan.)

Thousands were on hand when the Senators' train pulled in from Boston. A reporter noticed Joe Judge grimacing; he was reading a New York newspaper that had already declared the Giants to be the likely winners of the Series. The reporter asked Judge what had made the difference in the final stretch of the regular season. "Nerve," Judge replied.

Then he pointed to the article. Referring to the man who wrote it as "a trained seal," Joe made a prediction: "This bird is going to be a lot wiser, but sadder, when the series is over," he said.

5

A TEST OF CHARACTER

On October 1, 1924, an estimated one hundred thousand
people showed up for the parade along Pennsylvania
Avenue—the "Boulevard of Base Ball," as the old-time players
had known it—to honor the new American League champions.
There were mounted police, the U.S. Cavalry Band, politicians,
even the Washington Riding and Hunt Club. "The joy of the
cheering crowd was boundless," the *Washington Post* reported.
"Ten of the city's most beautiful young girls, dressed in white
and mounted on white horses," led a line of limousines carrying the members of the Senators team. Fans called out to the
players and flowers rained down on Walter Johnson as female
admirers blew him kisses.

At the Ellipse, President Coolidge presented the team with
a cup and a gold key to the city. That evening, two hundred of
the city's business, civic and professional leaders threw a ban-
quet. It was dry; even personal flasks were banned. ("The World
Series will not be lost here tonight!" one temperance-minded
bigwig harrumphed.)

His eyes glistening with tears, Clark Griffith made a speech:

> My blood is tingling and to say I'm proud is putting it awfully
> mild. This team is the gamest ball club I ever saw. It has met
> every crisis. When I came in the old days and sunk my mea-
> ger capital in the town, I was called a fool. But I always had
> Walter Johnson to lean on.

Yet even while the city was in a frenzy, Washingtonians were well aware that the Giants were one of the toughest teams of all time. An article in the *Washington Star* well expressed the general feeling:

> [The city's] fervent prayer and its undeniable determination is to walk straight into the most sanctum sanctorums of the baseball world over the bewildered forms of some hapless Giants before those hearties know what it is all about. [But] Washington fans began to realize this morning [Oct. 2] that tiring celebrations would not win the game. Yesterday this city was a pulsating throng of hilarious kids—kids ranging in age from 3 to 90—yelling themselves hoarse trying to make the returning Griffmen realize how proud their home city is of them. Today it has sobered down to the thought of that gigantic battle Saturday, and it is beginning to steel itself for the initial test.

The oddsmakers were calling the series a tossup, though on paper the Giants may have had a slight edge. Frederick G. Lieb, president of the Baseball Writers Association, considered the Giants infield "the best in baseball." First baseman Long George Kelly hit .324—the same as his Washington counterpart, Joe Judge—and led the majors with 136 RBIs. Second baseman Frankie Frisch, the Giants captain, hit .321 and scored 121 runs. Rookie third baseman Freddie Lindstrom, then eighteen years old, was a future Hall of Famer.

Lindstrom had movie star looks and a mordant sense of humor. Once, when the other Giants were griping about the hotels and food on a road trip, Lindstrom was asked why he wasn't joining in. He replied, "When a fellow is hitting .240, whatever he gets is much too good for him." Like everyone else, Lindstrom had run-ins with John McGraw. When Lindstrom broke his leg later in the 1920s, the Little Napoleon visited him at the hospital and, after some friendly words, began berating his third baseman for being careless. Lindstrom fired back that he hoped McGraw broke *his* leg. When the manager rushed angrily out of the hospital a few minutes later, he was knocked down by a taxi, fulfilling Lindstrom's wish.

In right field was Ross Youngs, who at .356 was the third-best hitter in the National League, with his eighth-year batting average over .300. In left field was Emil "Irish" Meusel, who drove in 102 runs in 1924 and would finish his career with a .310 average. Rookie center fielder Hack Wilson, another future Hall of Famer, was a perfect fit for McGraw at 5'6" and 195 pounds, with a size 18 collar and gigantic legs and shoulders. Wilson had dropped out of school in the sixth grade and worked in a locomotive factory and shipyard. And also like McGraw, Wilson was quick to use his fists, once decking two Cincinnati players in the same day—one at the park, the other that night at a train stop.

Hack's real name was Lew, but when a teammate said that Wilson reminded him of Hack Miller, the son of a famous circus strongman, the name stuck. He developed a personality to match it. One of his managers, desperate to keep the hard-drinking Wilson out of trouble during Prohibition, said to him, "If I drop a worm in a glass of water it just swims around. But if I drop it in a glass of whiskey, the worm dies. What does that prove?" Hack came back with: "It proves that if you drink whiskey you'll never get worms." As one writer punned, "On the field or in all night roistering, [Wilson] dispatched high balls with a prowess unknown to lesser mortals."

When Wilson first came to the Giants in 1923, there was some concern that his fireplug shape might make it hard to find a uniform to fit him. Reaching into his locker, McGraw pulled out a uniform and tossed it to Wilson. "Don't disgrace this uniform," McGraw said. "It was once worn by a great player."

"Who?" Wilson asked.

"Me," McGraw said.

Wilson would hit 56 home runs in 1930, a National League record for 68 years until it was surpassed by Mark McGwire.

The Senators could match the Giants in almost every category. In the miraculous 1924 season Goose Goslin hit .394 with 12 homers and 129 RBIs. Sam Rice hit .334, with 216 hits, 106 runs and 24 stolen bases. In addition to his .324 average, Joe Judge had 79 RBIs. And of course, the Senators had the pitching combination of Walter Johnson and Fred Marberry. Johnson was 23–7 in 1924 with an ERA of 2.72, and he had 158 strike-outs; he even batted .283. Marberry had pitched in 50 games in 1924, saving 15 of them. The rest of the pitching staff stacked up pretty evenly against New York. Washington had Tom Zachary (15–9), George Mogridge (16–11) and Curly Ogden (9–5) against the Giants' Art Nehf (14–4), Virgil Barnes (16–10), Jack Bentley (16–5) and Hugh McQuillan (14–8).

There were, however, a couple of categories where the Giants had a clear edge. The Senators had hit a mere 22 home runs the entire season—only one more than George Kelly alone had hit for the Giants. And New York had more depth on the bench and World Series experience: Frisch, Youngs, Kelly, Nehf and Meusel had played together in the three previous World Series. Another advantage was that for most of the season, the Giants had been comfortably on top and able to relax, while the American League had been a dogfight from Opening Day onward.

The Senators were clearly tired. "By the end of that season we were all worn down," Ossie Bluege recalled. "We all looked like scarecrows. We knew we'd been in a fight." Bucky Harris had been playing with a broken bone in his foot for two months; Ossie Bluege had a gimpy leg that team trainer Mike Martin had to wrap before every game; shortstop Roger Peckinpaugh had played in all 155 games of the season; Goslin and Rice had each missed only one game; while catcher Muddy Ruel's weight had dropped from 150 to 130 pounds, about which, in an interview with *Baseball* magazine, he had this to say:

> I have a rather slender build; I'm not one of these human truck horses that can stand anything. That cramping, crouching position tends to tie a man's legs into knots.... I don't feel the physical strain as much as the mental strain. A catcher really carries a heavy load. There's much more resting on his shoulders than on the shoulders of the shortstop or the first baseman. They're looking for a possible play that doesn't happen. The catcher is looking for a possible play that comes with every pitched ball.

This articulate ballplayer went on to record that his greatest problem was not knowing the Giants players as well as those of his own league: "The series is all too short to learn how to handle a dangerous batter." He would have an episode of bad slump during the Series, yet redeem himself spectacularly before the end.

On October 1, sportswriter Robert T. Small pithily summed up the differences between McGraw and Harris and their teams:

> Here are the opposing personalities of the World Series: one is gray-haired, a little too stoutish about the waistline, a veteran of 51 and acknowledged peer of any strategist the game has ever known. The other is a dark-haired youth, who hasn't played major league ball half as many years as his hated opponent has won pennants.

Small noted that whereas the 1923 Series, dominated by Ruth, was when "brute force beat mastermind," 1924 would be "mastermind against youth and courage and pluck and daring."

As for Ruth, he was pulling for the Senators. So was Ty Cobb, who said the Senators were "inbred with competitive spirit and they'll fight hard." Cobb also undoubtedly had a soft spot for his friend Walter Johnson, which caused him to act supportively. For Cobb had discovered how to hit Johnson, and had he given his secret to the Giants, the Senators might well have lost. By 1915 Cobb had had a lifetime average of .222 against the Big Train when, on August 10, a Johnson pitch struck one of the Tigers' batters, third baseman Ossie Vitt, on the forehead. Johnson momentarily thought he had killed the man, who escaped with a concussion. With his hallmark capacity for empathy, he was so shaken by what happened that he pitched the worst game of the season, giving up four runs in the first inning and four more over the next five before being relieved by Sam Rice.

Watching all this was Ty Cobb, who made a clever deduction: Johnson—with an arm like Zeus's but with the temperament of a Thomas Aquinas—was mortally afraid of injuring batters. So he began to crowd the plate, knowing that Johnson would throw outside. Yet when the pitcher got behind in the count, Cobb would return to his normal stance. Cobb later admitted that he was "cheating," but he had felt desperate. "I had to do something to get base hits against Johnson," he told sports-writer Shirley Povich in 1940. "He was making it too tough for me." From 1915 to 1936 Cobb averaged .435 against the Big Train.

While Cobb kept his mouth shut about his secret strategy, he did let something slip in a pre-Series interview that annoyed Babe Ruth: "I didn't win the pennant, but I had the consolation of kicking the Yankees out of the race, and I got quite a kick out of that." Ruth immediately responded:

> I see where [Cobb] gets a lot of happiness out of beating the Yankees in those three games that lost us the pennant. I also see where he's coming up from Georgia to do some World Series writing. Maybe he's going to say some more things to make the Yankees feel bad. And maybe, as he did so much toward Washington winning the pennant, he's coming to claim a share of the gate receipts from Clark Griffith.

The feud between the titans didn't last long. Sportswriter Christy Walsh tricked the two men into the same Washington cab on the way to the first game, and they soon made up. They spent most of the Series in the press box together, smoking cigars and swapping yarns.

$$\mathcal{O}$$

As THE DAY OF THE first game approached, the city of Washington began to seethe with anticipation. For those who couldn't get tickets, there was radio. Western Union had laid down 75,000 miles of cable to carry the game on scoreboards around the country. WRC radio in Washington would broadcast the games with Graham McNamee, who had once been a professional singer, doing play-by-play. Billy Roberts, a young boy living in Georgetown, became momentarily famous by using his radio, large pieces of translucent paper, a flashlight and a chalkboard to create his own diamond and scoreboard. He and his friends set up the board on his front porch, and it soon began to attract a crowd, "drawing from all parts of the neighborhood, white and black, young and old." The *Star* reported that one elderly black man arrived with his rocking chair, and when Billy's mother came home and saw the crowd, she thought there had been a fire.

On Friday, October 3, the Senators took the field for their final workout. It may have been difficult to concentrate—in the outfield, workmen were hammering together the last of the makeshift bleachers that Griffith had installed for the Series. The ticket office was being overrun by people desperate for the last two thousand tickets. Head ticket man Ed Enyon had worked himself to exhaustion and was surrounded by six policemen. At least two fans would succeed in getting into the game free. The first was "One-Eyed" Connolly, famous for crashing sporting events; he was given a job selling programs. The second was a boy who managed to sneak into the park three times until the policeman chasing him finally gave up.

In the midst of all the chaos, a story broke that threatened the Series itself. Commissioner Landis had heard there had been a bribe attempt by one of the Giants at the end of the season, when the team's once-huge lead had shrunk to one-and-a-half games over Brooklyn. A three-game series with the Phillies could have ended New York's season. On September 27, so the allegation went, Giants outfielder Jimmy O'Connell offered Phillies shortstop Heinie Sand $500 to take it easy. Sand rejected the offer and reported the incident to Brooklyn manager Art Fletcher. The news was taken to Commissioner Landis, and Jimmy O'Connell claimed that Giants Frankie Frisch, Ross Youngs and George Kelly were in on the plan. O'Connell fingered Giants coach Cozy Dolan as mastermind of the plot.

Immediately, the American League president and John McGraw's nemesis, Ban Johnson, demanded that the Series be cancelled. He was overruled by Landis and the baseball advisory council—there was just too much interest around the country in seeing Walter Johnson play in a World Series. O'Connell and Dolan, however, would be banned from baseball for life as a result of the scandal.

October 4 was an Indian summer day in Washington, and the stands began to fill up early at Griffith Stadium for game one. "The stands were just packed with notables," recalled Walter Johnson's wife, Hazel. "You couldn't have thrown a ball without hitting an ambassador or senator or a cabinet officer or famous writer or an actor or prize fighter or some other distinguished individual." The most famous was Calvin Coolidge, who arrived with the First Lady and sat in a flag-draped section near the Senators' dugout. With him in the box were the secretary of war, the secretary of state and the Speaker of the House.

Preparing for the biggest game of his life, Walter Johnson had a bad case of the jitters. "I am doggone fidgety about my job this afternoon," he told Babe Ruth that morning. "Especially when you figure every last soul in the ball park expects me to win, including the President of the United States." When umpire Billy Evans came in to have Johnson autograph a few balls, he noticed Johnson's hand shaking. Before the team went out, Bucky Harris put a hand on Johnson's shoulder. "The boys are going to fight extra hard to see you win," he said.

Out on the field, the U.S. Army Band was playing behind home plate while reporters crowded the diamond and the stands continued to fill up. Johnson and Sam Rice tried to loosen up by playing catch, but the press of cameramen made it impossible. So Johnson attempted to make his way to the bench, but was met by more well-wishers, among them Babe Ruth, who was busy offering advice on pitching to Giants batters.

Suddenly, Joe Judge rushed up. "They're looking all over for you," he yelled to Johnson. Judge pointed to home plate, where there was a new seven-passenger Lincoln car—at $8,000 the most expensive automobile then made in the United States. It was decorated with a gigantic floral horseshoe, and on the dashboard was a silver plaque with the inscription: "To Walter Johnson, baseball's greatest pitcher, from his many friends." A committee of fans had formed to raise the money, with President Coolidge contributing ten dollars.

Johnson, as usual, endured the attention stoically. Almost the only good thing about the ceremony, he said later, was that "it was at home plate. I was getting closer to the pitcher's box. And the closer I got, the better I felt." The Giants, however, didn't seem impressed. Washington catcher Muddy Ruel remembered the Giants "looking at us with tolerance and amused confidence. . . . They had McGraw scowling from the bench." But Ruel was not intimidated. "They were an awesome club, but not to us. We Senators were tough, too."

After some more delays, the teams got ready to play. But there was one last thing: photographers wanted a picture of Johnson with Art Nehf, who would be pitching for New York. "I felt sorry for him when we shook hands," Nehf would recall, "because his hand trembled so. I knew what he was thinking. He was thinking he mustn't let down the fans all over the country who were rooting, even praying, for him."

At two o'clock, Walter Johnson took the mound to the cheers of forty thousand. He paused for a moment to acknowledge the crowd, then faced his first batter, 18-year-old rookie third baseman Freddie Lindstrom—born the same year Johnson had started playing in the majors. Lindstrom quickly flied out to Earl McNeely in center field. Frankie Frisch also flied out, and was followed by Ross Youngs, who struck out. The Senators then also went down in order, victims of Art Nehf and his sharp, sweeping curve.

In the second inning, things began to go badly for Washington. Leadoff batter George Kelly, working from a 3–2 count, drove a fastball into left center. Had Griffith not installed so many new bleachers, the ball would have been easily caught by Goslin. As it was, Goslin had to pull up in front of the three-foot fence guarding the new seats, then dive into the crowd to try and make the catch. The ball dropped inches from his mitt, giving New York a home run and a 1–0 lead.

The Senators got only one man on base in the bottom of the inning—Joe Judge on a walk. After a scoreless third inning the Giants struck again in the fourth. Pinch hitter and first baseman Bill Terry swung late on a fastball and drove the ball into the bleachers, near the same spot where George Kelly's homer had gone in the first inning.

Joe Judge got the first hit off Nehf in the fourth, but it was with two outs and he never got home. In the sixth, however, the rest of the Washington squad came to life. McNeely drove a double over third base and moved up to third when Harris grounded out. Sam Rice then hit a slow grounder to second, bringing McNeely home. "Was there any clamor?" Grantland Rice would write of the crowd's reaction. "Was Babel quiet? Our ears are still throbbing." The Giants' lead was now 2–1.

For the next three innings, the teams were deadlocked, relying on great pitching and tough defense. In the top of the seventh, the Senators escaped a potential Giants rally with "a lightning fast double play that electrified the crowd." The Giants responded in the bottom of the inning when, with two men on, Johnson hit a line drive that was headed to right field until it was hooked by second baseman Frisch. In the eighth, the Giants had men on first and third and attempted a double steal; Muddy Ruel fooled the runner by holding on to the ball for an extra moment, then firing to third instead of second.

The Senators' last chance to tie the game came in the ninth. They had prevented the Giants from adding to their lead at the top of the inning on a bullet fired to the plate by Rice to cut off a run. But they needed a run to tie. Judge didn't help, watching a third strike to lead off. But then Ossie Bluege blasted a shot at the hole that shortstop Travis Jackson could only knock down. Peckinpaugh followed with a double off the wall in left center, bringing in Bluege and tying the game.

Grantland Rice described the crowd's reaction as "the cyclonic thunder of the day ... the crashing artillery of 38,000 voices in one of the wildest vocal frenzies anyone ever heard." Thousands of hats and cushions went onto the field, and the game was held up for several minutes. Even the usually phlegmatic Calvin Coolidge, chain-smoking cigars, jumped up several times to applaud.

The game went into extra innings. In the bottom of the tenth, with Sam Rice and Bucky Harris on first and second, Judge brought the crowd to its feet with a blast to deep right that drove Ross Youngs back to the wall, but Youngs made the catch. Then, in the top of the twelfth, Johnson hit Hank Gowdy with a pitch. With Gowdy on first, the next batter, pitcher Art Nehf, sent a lazy pop fly into shallow center field. Earl McNeely, the late-season replacement for Wid Mathews, misjudged the ball, waiting a few crucial seconds before charging. He had the ball in the webbing of his glove for a moment but tumbled, the ball popping loose as he hit the ground. When he got to his feet and saw Gowdy stranded between first and second, he hurled wildly to second, sending the ball over the head of Harris and almost into the Giants' dugout. Gowdy pulled up at third, Nehf stopping at second.

McGraw then sent up pitcher Jack Bentley to hit. Bentley had played with the Senators from 1912 to 1916, but was let go when his arm faltered. He was released to the Baltimore Orioles, where he reincarnated himself as a power hitter and outfielder. Miraculously, in 1920 his arm came back and he went 16–3 with a 2.11 ERA and a .371 batting average. In 1922 he was sold to the Giants and became one of the best pinch hitters in the majors.

Johnson intentionally walked Bentley, loading the bases. McGraw then sent in Billy Southworth, one of his fastest players, to run for Bentley. The next batter, Frankie Frisch, grounded to Harris, who forced Gowdy out at home. Then Ross Youngs hit a soft floater to center, but McNeely was again slow coming in for the ball. It dropped for a single, and Nehf scored. The next batter, George Kelly, drove a fly to Goslin in left field, and Southworth tagged up from third. The Senators avoided disaster when a diving Joe Judge speared a hot grounder from Bill Terry, but Judge couldn't get to his feet in time to beat Terry to first base. The bases were loaded for the fourth time of the inning. Luckily, the next batter, Hack Wilson, flied out to Goslin. The Giants were up 4–2 going into the bottom of the twelfth.

Harris sent in Mule Shirley to bat for Johnson, and Shirley got on base when shortstop Travis Jackson fumbled a pop-up. McNeely then flied out, and Harris drove a ball deep enough into center (this was endless Griffith Stadium after all) to bring Shirley home from first. Sam Rice came up next, smashing a pitch to the same spot. Harris pulled up at third and Rice unwisely tried to stretch the hit into a double. He was easily thrown out. Two outs.

Goose Goslin, the Senators' best hitter, came up with Joe Judge on deck. He hit a slow roller to George Kelly, who was temporarily playing second base. Harris crossed home and Kelly threw Goose out, according to one report, by "an eyelash." To the Senators—and everyone in Griffith Stadium—it appeared obvious that Harris had crossed home before Goose was thrown out. (In 1924, if a runner scored before a third out was made, the run counted.) But umpire Bill Klem ruled otherwise.

The Senators went crazy. Mild, amiable Joe Judge, the cool "sheet anchor" of the Washington Senators, charged over from the on-deck circle and joined Goslin, Harris and Nick Altrock, who were surrounding Klem. Goslin called Klem "Catfish," a nickname the umpire couldn't stand. (Klem would never forgive Goose, even when years later he tried to apologize.) The other players backed off, but Judge kept arguing, following the umpire off the field. They were just ahead of Calvin Coolidge, and when the president passed by Judge and Klem, the bickering pair didn't even notice.

Even after such a heartbreaking loss, the Senators remained defiant. "Tomorrow is another day," said Bucky Harris, "It's the first time I ever saw the Giants in action in a World Series, and I really believe that we have the better team and will go on to win the World Championship."

♫

WALTER JOHNSON HAD THROWN 165 pitches in the first game, including 12 strikeouts, tying a World Series record. He said he had tried his "level best" and he had "no excuses." He also said he wasn't angry at McNeely for booting the ball in center field and then compounding the error by throwing wildly. "No one should blame the boy," Johnson said. "He was just overanxious, that's all."

The next morning before the second game, Johnson visited disabled soldiers at Walter Reed Hospital to bring them all the flowers left over from the opening game. "Despite the sad surroundings," he would remember, "the situation was amusing. I was sorry for the boys and they were sorry for me. They hesitated talking about my lost game as one might avoid mentioning some poor lad's missing arm or leg." One veteran wasn't so quiet, however. He insisted on being pushed down to Johnson in his wheelchair. He couldn't shake hands because, as Johnson noted, he didn't have any hands. "Barney, we all know how you feel," the man said, using one of the pitcher's nicknames. "A guy's a hero today and a dud tomorrow. Cheer up!"

Despite the previous day's loss, the atmosphere for the second game at Griffith Stadium was festive, even jubilant. The weather was perfect. "Not a shadow to mar the blue of that great dome above," a reporter wrote. "A gentle wind, a warm and mellow sun, a great wall of moving color steeped high in mass, a wall around the green of the grassy playing field below." The Meyer Goldwyn Band took the field at eleven o'clock, playing standards like "My Old Kentucky Home" as well as some jazz tunes. The peanut vendors, dressed in white, saw the bleachers filling up early and took off across the field towards them in a stampede that one witness compared to a military assault. Comedian Nick Altrock then appeared, asking the band to play Chopin's "Funeral March" in honor of the Giants. He marched up and down the stands to the music and, at the end of the piece, lay down and "died."

McGraw started another left-handed pitcher, former Senator Jack Bentley. McGraw's strategy was to use the big southpaw to shut down Washington's best hitters, lefties Goslin, Rice and Judge. This strategy backfired in the very first inning, when Rice singled, then stole second. He was followed by Goslin, who homered into the right-field bleachers.

After giving up two singles in the first, Senators pitcher Tom Zachary bore down, giving up only one more hit going into the seventh. He got some insurance when Harris homered in the fifth, giving Washington a 3–0 lead.

The Giants did not fold, however. Zachary walked George Kelly to lead off the seventh, then Irish Meusel singled, sending Kelly to third. Hack Wilson grounded into a double play, scoring Kelly. The Senators got the next two Giants out, keeping their 3–1 lead going into the ninth.

Zachary walked Frankie Frisch to open the inning and was followed by Ross Youngs, who popped out. Kelly then singled to right field and Sam Rice juggled the ball, his throw coming half a second too late to get Frisch at the plate. Only a brilliant stop by Harris on a grounder to the right side of the infield got Washington its second out as Kelly moved up to second. The next batter, Hack Wilson, singled to right, driving in Kelly with the tying run.

Harris called for Fred Marberry, who had led the American League with fifteen saves. He struck out Travis Jackson to end the inning.

Joe Judge led off the bottom of the ninth. After "fouling several balls viciously," as one paper put it the next day, he drew a walk. Ossie Bluege then laid down a sacrifice bunt, sending Judge to second. Peckinpaugh was next up. He sent a line drive over third baseman Freddie Lindstrom's head and down the left-field line. Judge got home easily with the winning run in a 4–3 victory.

The Washington fans went into a paroxysm. The field became such a wild scene that Peckinpaugh almost didn't make it to the clubhouse. Hundreds of fans—"not all of whom were boys or men," reported the *Star*—refused to leave the area around the clubhouse until some of the players came out to take a bow. One fan, who had bought his tickets from a scalper at an exorbitant price, evidently reckoned he had gotten his money's worth: he left the park shouting, "Anybody who thinks these two games have not been worth fifty dollars is a goat!"

The Senators were heartened by the victory. On the special "baseball car" of the train taking them to New York, they exuded a new confidence to reporters. "It's not in the books for us to be beaten here this year," one player said. The team had not lost a series in New York all year. They had beaten the Yankees two out of three games early in the season, then four straight in June and three out of four again in August. For the Giants, the Polo Grounds seemed jinxed. They had not won a World Series game at home since 1922. Still, the Associated Press noted that 15 of the last 20 World Series had been won by the team that had won the first game.

There would be changes in the New York lineups for the third game. Bill Terry, the Giant's left-handed slugger whose bat had been crucial to their victory in game one but who had trouble in the second game hitting against southpaw Zachary, would play first, sending George Kelly to center field. McGraw hoped Terry would have better luck against right-handed reliever Fred Marberry, who was starting for the Senators.

The Polo Grounds was an oddly configured, V-shaped park: 279 feet to the left-field fence, 257 to right and a whopping 484 feet to deepest center. For players who pulled balls to the left or right, it was a dream; for those who hit straightaway, a nightmare. Warming up before game three, left-handers Goslin and Judge eyed the close right-field fence. "That right-field stand is just my dish," Goose told the Associated Press. "They must have built it for me." Joe added, "I've put a few in there myself."

Judge didn't make any homers in game three, but he did have three hits—including a double in the fourth that drove in two runs. But this was one of the few highlights in a game the Senators lost 6–4. It was, everyone on both teams and in the media agreed, the worst game in the series. Washington's infield simply broke down. Roger Peckinpaugh had hurt his right leg after his game-winning single in the second game, and by the third inning of game three he was in so much pain he had to come out. Before the game, Harris had wanted to substitute an unknown named Tommy Taylor for third baseman Ossie Bluege, who would move to shortstop. But Taylor had a splint on his throwing hand, which had been hurt—or so it was believed—by punching someone's head the night the Senators won the pennant in Boston. At the last minute, Harris had asked Peckinpaugh to do his best.

But now Peck was out and so was his backup. Harris was forced to put the poor-fielding Ralph Miller in at third, moving Bluege to shortstop. Miller had played in only three games all year. In the sixth inning, he "let a sorry-hit grounder pass completely through his quaking legs," as one newspaper reported. Miller wasn't the only soft spot for the Senators, however. In the second inning Harris dropped a double-play ball, allowing New York to score two runs. Both teams burned through four pitchers. The Senators left thirteen men on base.

"I cannot say that I am proud of that ball game," John McGraw wrote in his syndicated column. "Stanley Harris, I'm sure, will agree with me. Of all the bad pitching in a World Series game, when taken as a whole, that was the worst."

The loss of Peckinpaugh spelt doom for the Senators—or so thought Baseball Writers Association president Frederick G. Lieb. He had called Peck the best player on Washington's team. Ralph Miller was, he wrote, "a poor substitute" and "a mediocre player." Moreover, Walter Johnson, so as to give his aging arm one more day of rest, was not going to pitch the fourth game.

Lieb didn't reckon on Goose Goslin and the Senators' bullpen. Around Washington for years, game four was referred to as "the Goose Goslin game." Things got off to a shaky start in the first inning, when an error by Ossie Bluege at his unaccustomed position allowed a run to score. But then Goslin, who had been 3 for 15 in the first three games, suddenly woke up. Having already gotten a hit in the second, he came up in the third with two out and McNeely and Harris on base. He jumped at the first pitch offered by Virgil Barnes, slamming it into the right-field grandstand.

With the score 4–1 Washington in the fifth, Goose got his third hit in the game, driving Harris home from second. He led off the eighth with another hit, and he and Joe Judge came home on a single by Ossie Bluege.

If Goslin was brilliant, so was Washington's pitcher, the 35-year-old George Mogridge, who gave up only three hits. Mogridge was up 7–2 in the seventh when he was relieved by Marberry, who gave up two runs but then struck out both Jack Bentley and George Kelly in the bottom of the ninth.

The Series was now tied at two games each. Another victory in New York would mean that the Senators would return home with a 3–2 lead. In this tense situation, Walter Johnson was slated to pitch the fifth game. One of the first things the Big Train did was ask the injured Roger Peckinpaugh to play; he just didn't like the new infield configuration of Miller at third and Bluege at shortstop. Peckinpaugh could barely move, but Johnson told him that he didn't care—to have him in the infield in any condition would be worth it. Peck had to refuse. He simply could not run.

The day of the fifth game was sunny and cool, the field fresh from an overnight rain. The day began promisingly for Washington. As the Big Train headed for the mound, the crowd erupted in applause in what one AP reporter called "a vocal tribute from Manhattan Island to the old speed king."

The Senators' first batter, Earl McNeely, smashed a pitch from Jack Bentley, only to have third baseman Freddie Lindstrom make a spectacular leaping catch to rob him of what would have been an extra-base hit. It was an omen of things to come.

Johnson was coasting in the third inning when he made a rookie mistake. The game was still scoreless when he came up to the plate, receiving another ovation from the crowd. (Grantland Rice estimated that 80 percent of New York was rooting for Johnson.) He drove a pitch against the left-field wall. Thinking he had an easy double, Johnson was on his way to second base when he looked up and realized that Giants outfielder Hack Wilson had played the carom off the wall perfectly and was already throwing back to infield. Johnson tried to head back to first, but it was too late. Jackson's toss to Frisch was relayed to first and Johnson was tagged out. McNeely and Harris both followed with singles, but both were left on base and the Senators failed to score.

In the bottom of the inning, Peckinpaugh's absence would once again cost Washington. The Giants' Travis Jackson hit a grounder to third that went under the glove of Ralph Miller, who at this point was probably wondering, along with thousands of fans, how he had ever made it into the majors, much less a World Series. Luckily, shortstop Ossie Bluege had backed Miller up, and Jackson was held to a single. Hank Gowdy struck out next, but he was followed by pitcher Jack Bentley, who singled to right, sending Jackson to third. The next batter, Freddie Lindstrom, topped a pitch, sending it trickling slowly down the third baseline. Miller came in on the ball timidly, missing a chance to get either Jackson out at home or Lindstrom at first.

There were now runners on first and second with Frankie Frisch at the plate. Frisch grounded to Bluege, who threw to Miller at third. Instead of touching the bag for the force out, Miller tried to tag Bentley coming from second and missed. This loaded the bases for Ross Youngs, who smashed a line drive to right field. Sam Rice caught the ball and fired to Johnson, who relayed to Muddy Ruel in time to tag Bentley, who had tried to tag from third. Sam's double play had averted a potential disaster, although the Giants were on top, 1–0.

Joe Judge led off the top of the fourth with a single to the right-field wall. He went to second on a sacrifice by Bluege, then took third when Muddy Ruel grounded to short. Next up was Ralph Miller, a disaster in the field and 1–7 at the plate for the series so far. Miller drove the ball down the right-field line, easily scoring Judge. But Miller, perhaps intoxicated with his moment of glory, tried to stretch the play into a double and was gunned down easily by Youngs.

Beginning in the bottom of the fourth, Johnson began to weaken. He was lucky to get out of the inning after Bill Terry, with one out, drove a ball 484 feet to the center-field wall of the Polo Grounds. John McGraw called the triple "the longest line hit I ever saw made at the Polo Grounds; the ball hit the fence on a line at the furthest point from the plate in deep center." But Terry would never make it home, getting doubled off the bag at third when the next batter, Travis Jackson, drove a line drive back to Johnson.

In the bottom of the fifth Hank Gowdy singled, then Jack Bentley put the Giants ahead 3–1 by popping over the short right-field wall—an easy-out fly ball in any other park. Once again the Senators infield held back the flood. A Bluege-to-Harris-to-Judge double play got them out of the inning. The infield also saved them in the seventh. With two outs, and Freddie Lindstrom on third and Ross Youngs on first, McGraw called for a double steal. If Lindstrom could make it home before Youngs was tagged out at second, the run would count. Youngs took off from first and Muddy Ruel fired to Harris at second. Youngs stopped and headed back to first. Harris fired to Judge, who, keeping his eye on Lindstrom at third, chased Youngs back towards second. Judge relayed the ball back to Harris, who saw Lindstrom take off for home. Harris fired home to Ruel, who tagged Lindstrom in the nick of time.

The eighth inning started well for the Senators when Goose Goslin hit his third home run of the series, tying a record set by Babe Ruth. (Goslin's earlier hit in the second inning was his sixth in a row; it's still a World Series record.) But that was all Washington got, and when the Giants came up in the bottom of the ninth, things began to come apart for good. George Kelly singled and Bill Terry walked. Hack Wilson bunted, and Johnson fumbled the ball, loading the bases. Hugh Jackson hit a sacrifice fly to left, scoring Kelly. Hank Gowdy grounded to Miller, who forced Wilson at second, leaving men at first and third with two outs. Pitcher Hugh McQuillan then dropped a blooper into left field, scoring Terry. Then Freddie Lindstrom tagged Johnson for New York's thirteenth hit of the game and Gowdy scored. It was 6–2 New York.

Watching the Senators disintegrate, the crowd at the Polo Grounds grew quiet. A writer for the Associated Press described the scene:

> As the dying shadows of a chill October day crept down from Logan's Bluff, Walter Johnson stood on the mound of the Polo Grounds taking his punishment without a murmur. There was a spirit of the dying gladiator in the air. The stands were silent; the spectators were stunned.

But as Henry W. Thomas, Walter Johnson's grandson, relates in his superb book *Walter Johnson: Baseball's Big Train,* not everyone in the stands was silent. As Johnson was getting rocked, one man began to shout, "Take him out! Take him out!" Sitting in the same section was umpire Billy Evans, who had been rooting for Washington the entire Series. Evans charged the man, yelling to the other fans also going after him, "Let him alone, let me have him. He's mine." The irate spectators had wanted to pummel the heckler, but wound up having to save him from Evans. Later Evans would explain himself: "I can stand for anything they call me when I'm out there, but it seemed a shame to razz a man like Walter, who was in there giving everything he had. It hurt to have someone shout out that old line."

Reporters were tough on both Johnson and Harris the next day. "Trying to fulfill the hopes of the nation," John Keller wrote in the *Star,* "Johnson overpitched himself.... He toiled not confident in himself but fearing defeat that would disappoint the many fans who had waited to see him in baseball's classic." But Damon Runyon was more elegiac in his newspaper column:

> A bright vision hung and held for just a moment over the Polo Grounds this afternoon—the vision of a tall, fresh-cheeked, fair-haired, brawny youth pitching with power, with blinding, dazzling speed. It was just a mirage of older years. Now it has vanished, the youth was gone. By some tragic quirk of the imagination there stood in his place an old fellow with

stooping shoulders, as if they felt the great weight of years. . . . Almost mercifully the evening shadows closed over the stooped shoulders in the ninth inning, as he slowly trudged toward the distant clubhouse, keeping close to the walls above which sat the raging crowd.

In the locker room after the game, Johnson slumped in front of his locker with his head in his hands. Players tried to cheer him up, but as Muddy Ruel remembered, "nothing could rouse him from his depression." Muddy put his arm around Johnson and tried to console him.

"Muddy," Johnson said, "I would have cut off my right arm to win that ball game today. But I failed. And I've failed twice."

"Never mind, old man," Ruel told his friend. "You'll beat 'em yet! This series isn't over yet, not by a long shot."

Griffith also tried to offer Johnson some encouragement on the quiet train ride back to Washington:

Don't think about it anymore, Walter. You're a great pitcher. We all know it. Now tonight when we get home, don't stand around the box office buying seats for friends or shaking hands with people who feel sorry for you. Go home and get to bed early. We may need you.

WALTER'S DAY

The news wasn't all bleak for Washington. At the end of the fifth game, Commissioner Landis summoned Bucky Harris and John McGraw to his box for a coin toss to decide the venue for the seventh game. The Little Napoleon called heads and it came up tails. "Well, you win," was all he said to his old rival. So the final game, if needed, would be played at Griffith Stadium.

On the subdued train home, the Senators were still defiant. During the ride, Giants catcher Hank Gowdy came to the Senators' car for a visit. Striking up a conversation with Lawrence Phillips, the announcer at Griffith Stadium, Gowdy claimed to be delighted at going back to Washington, where the baseball crowds were "fine." He then asked Phillips if he thought there would be a big turnout for Thursday's game. "Sure," Phillips replied, "and there'll be a big one for Friday's, too."

To the team's surprise, some five thousand fans were waiting when the Senators' train pulled into Union Station. Recollecting the encouragement they gave the players as they disembarked that evening, Walter Johnson later wrote:

> The cheering made one's blood tingle. That display of loyalty at midnight, totally unexpected after we had failed to win, acted like a powerful stimulant. The spirit of our ball club changed overnight.

Roger Peckinpaugh was back at shortstop for game six with his leg wrapped so tightly by trainer Mike Martin that he almost couldn't feel his foot touch the ground. With Peck playing short, Ossie Bluege was able to go back to third. The Giants' first batter, Freddie Lindstrom, tested the reconfigured infield with a bunt; Ossie quickly mowed him down. Frankie Frisch followed with a double down the right-field line; then Ross Youngs hit a grounder back to pitcher Tom Zachary, who trapped Frisch in a rundown while Youngs moved to second. George Kelly then singled, bringing home Ross. The inning ended only when Sam Rice made a difficult catch on a line drive by Irish Meusel.

It seemed as though the Giants batters had Zachary in their gun sights. But starting in the second inning, the quiet veteran found a groove. He allowed only five hits and one runner to get to second for the rest of the game; in fact, Zachary never threw more than two balls to any Giants batter.

Washington finally scored in the fifth inning. Peckinpaugh led off with a single—his second of the game—then moved up to second on a sacrifice by Ruel. Zachary grounded out, moving Peck up to third with two out. Center fielder Earl McNeely then drew a walk, which brought up Bucky Harris. On the first pitch, McNeely took off for second, attempting a steal.

This could have been a catastrophic play. After all, the Senators had the hamstrung Peckinpaugh, unable to take any chances, on third. Had McNeely been thrown out, it would have ended the inning. But he beat the throw from catcher Hank Gowdy by a whisker and was called safe. Bucky Harris then drove in both runners with a shot to right.

The final score was 2–1 Senators. *Baseball* magazine fulsomely described how much hinged on that stolen base:

> A flash of time: a fraction of a second: a single step, or the slowness of that step—such things have uncrowned kings, wrecked empires, won pennants, sealed the championship of the world. The highest honors of the game, in the sixth great battle, balance swaying in the scales, and one step turned defeat to victory. When Earl McNeely stole second base in the fifth inning, the fate of that ball-game hung in mid-air as the ball swept down and the plunging runner slid. The tiniest

space of time; the slightest hesitation, meant the third out, and meant that the New York Giants were champions of the world.

They may be champions yet—tied up, three and three, another game is slated for the coming afternoon, and New York may win. If the Giants do come through, their final triumph was delayed a day; if they fall by the wayside, that one fast step, that flashing pulse of time, was what held them back and gave Washington the chance to beat them down. In any and all events, that running slide, that triumph over time and Gowdy's arrow throw, meant a fortune to the rival ball-clubs, a golden fortune that comes with the final game.

The Senators' victory came at a cost, however. In the top of the ninth, the Giants had one man on first with one out, when Irish Meusel drove a ball towards center field. Peckinpaugh, who had been playing in the hole, managed to snag the ball. He flipped to Harris, who relayed to Judge on one bounce. Almost simultaneously, two men went down—Peckinpaugh and Judge. Peck had landed on his bad leg, and after making the throw, he collapsed and had to be carried from the field by two teammates. Joe was luckier: Harris's throw had struck his knee but not damaged it. He would be back for the seventh game, but Peckinpaugh was through.

Hours after the end of the sixth game, Bucky Harris was in the Senators' locker room talking to Bryan Mores, city editor of the *Washington Herald,* and George P. Marshall, a prominent businessman. After swearing the men to silence, he outlined his plan for the seventh and final game of the World Series. Harris felt that the Giants' most dangerous offensive weapon was the rookie Bill Terry, who had 6 hits and 3 walks in 16 times at bat.

Terry had a well-known difficulty hitting left-handed pitchers, and McGraw tried to use him only against right-handers. Harris's idea was this: he would start the weak right-hander Curly Ogden, which meant that McGraw would put Terry in the line-up. Then Harris would switch, pulling Ogden after one batter and replacing him with lefty George Mogridge. McGraw could leave Terry in or yank him, but either way the Senators would have the edge. If Mogridge got rocked, Harris was willing to take his chances later with Marberry and even Johnson.

Harris went to clear the plan with Griffith. The Old Fox gave his approval, "even if it was a bit radical at first glance," as he later said; then he summoned the Big Train and outlined the plan, warning that he should be ready to pitch in the late innings. Johnson's wife, Hazel, who had been worrying that the pressure would be too much for her husband, broke down and cried.

Hazel's spirits were raised the morning of the game by a package that arrived at their house. Inside was a horseshoe wrapped in red, white and blue ribbons, along with a note from the baseball club of the Illinois State Penitentiary. They had sent "this lucky emblem and trust that it will live up to its tradition." Hazel brought it with her to the park.

$\mathcal{C}$

OCTOBER 10, 1924, WAS A perfect day, sunny and with an occasional breeze. It was the final day of the World Series, and the whole city of Washington was shut down. One reporter observed:

> The situation was truly remarkable. Government has been at a standstill; local business has been thrown out of joint; professional men have deserted their offices. Doctors waved away their patients and postponed important operations; dentists paid no heed to the pleas of persons howling with an aching tooth; lawyers excused themselves from all clients, and in the shops purchasers could get nowhere with the sales persons who were demanding to know the latest word from the thousands of radio sets scattered all over the city.

It was estimated that five thousand people were in line for the few tickets still available to the public.

But the balmy weather couldn't hide the exhaustion of the players, especially Walter Johnson. He had assured Hazel that morning that he was "primed for another battle," but she wasn't so sure, claiming her husband's courage was due to "willingness of spirit rather than strength of flesh." At first, she wanted to leave the stands entirely and sit in the car, but her companion, California congresswoman Mae Nolan, got her to stay—though only after Hazel insisted that they sit in the bleachers rather than the grandstand, just in case the tension got to her nerves and she needed to make a quick getaway. The entire game, she clutched the lucky horseshoe from her friends at the Illinois State Penitentiary.

After President Coolidge had said a few words, ending with the traditional "May the better team win," Curly Ogden took the mound for Washington. George Mogridge was out of sight under the stands, warming up. Freddie Lindstrom came up to bat, only to be struck out on three pitches. Curly began heading in toward the bench, but Harris sent him back: he didn't want to pull a pitcher who was hot.

But he walked the next batter, Frankie Frisch, and Harris called for the switch. George Mogridge came in, promptly striking out Ross Youngs and getting Kelly to ground out to Tommy Taylor, fielding at third.

The next few innings were dominated by powerful pitching—Mogridge doing the work for the Senators and Virgil Barnes for the Giants. But in the bottom of the fourth, Bucky Harris connected for one of the few home runs of his twelve-year career, driving a 3–2 pitch into the temporary left-field bleachers, the selfsame spot that many thought had caused the Senators' downfall in the first game. Left fielder Hack Wilson tried to clear a barricade to make the catch. The impact, in Grantland Rice's amusing simile, sounded "like a barrel of crockery being pushed down the cellar stairs." Hack was a little dazed as fans hoisted him back onto the field, but on the next play this tough man was able to make a spectacular diving catch of a line drive by Sam Rice.

When Bucky made his epic homer, the crowd rose as one—including that confirmed stoic, Calvin Coolidge, who "leapt up and beat his palms together in the sheer ecstasy of the moment," according to *Baseball* magazine. The Senators had struck first.

The defenses of both teams prevented any more runs until the top of the sixth, when George Mogridge began to slip. He walked leadoff batter Ross Youngs. The next batter, George Kelly, singled into center field, moving Youngs up to third. With a rally brewing, John McGraw decided to send in pinch hitter Irish Meusel to bat for Bill Terry, who had so far grounded out and struck out against the left-handed Mogridge. When McGraw made the switch, Harris did likewise, bringing in Marberry for Mogridge, who got standing applause as he left the field.

But the ovation had barely died down when another, louder one began, as a familiar figure emerged from the Washington dugout and headed for the right-field bullpen to warm up. Turning to the crowd, Walter Johnson waved. For the first time in two days, he smiled.

Irish Meusel sent a Marberry pitch to deep right field. Rice caught the ball, but Youngs tagged from third to tie the game. Hack Wilson followed with a single to center. There were now men on first and third.

The next play would be the worst in my grandfather's career. Giants shortstop Travis Jackson slapped a sharp grounder to first and he badly misplayed the ball. Judge, in the words of W. A. Phelon of *Baseball* magazine, "first fumbled and then dumbbelled," then "stood stock-still while Jackson ran by him." By the time he got control of the ball, Joe knew that the play at the plate was lost as Jackson made it to first and Wilson to second.

The next batter, Hank Gowdy, nailed a shot to short, and the ball went right through the legs of Ossie Bluege, who was unaccustomed to the position. "My worst error ever," Bluege would later claim, joining Judge in that regard. "I looked up at second base just before the ball got to me." Wilson scored and Jackson went to third. The Giants had the lead, 3–1. The inning ended on a fly to Rice and a strikeout.

In the seventh, the teams both went down quickly. The Giants went down almost in order in the top of the eighth. They were up by two runs, and the Senators would have only two more chances.

The first man up in the last of the eighth, Ossie Bluege, tipped a foul pop to catcher Hank Gowdy. But the next batter, Nemo Leibold, batting for Taylor, hooked a shot down the third-base line for a double. He was followed by Muddy Ruel, who hit a ball so sharply into short right field that the best play Kelly could make was to knock the ball down. Leibold moved to third. The Senators had men on first and third with one out.

The next batter was untested rookie backup catcher Bennie Tate, who was sent in to pinch-hit for Marberry. As Tate approached the batter's box, the attention of the fans was again drawn to the Senators' dugout. Walter Johnson was heading to the bullpen to warm up for the second time, but now he was rushing. The fans came to their feet, their cheers becoming a sustained roar as Tate drew a walk and Harris sent in Mule Shirley as a pinch runner.

With the bases loaded, Earl McNeely stepped to the plate for Washington. He took a ball, then hit a fly ball into left field. Two out.

Bucky Harris was up next. After Giants catcher Hank Gowdy went to the Giants' bench and consulted with McGraw, play resumed. Harris fought Barnes to a 2–2 count. Then he took two steps forward in the batter's box. Barnes threw a mean screwball, and Harris was trying to get out in front of it before it broke. He hit a grounder towards Lindstrom at third.

It was here that the first of the two miracles of the 1924 World Series occurred. The ball took a freak bounce, over Lindstrom's head and deep into left field. Leibold and Ruel scored, tying the game.

The crowd at Griffith Stadium couldn't contain itself. A few fans began spilling onto the field. Calvin Coolidge dropped his cigar. His wife, Grace, "jumped up and down on both feet, waved her arms, yelled, called out, and did all the other things that the fair fans were doing." The stadium was in "an uproar past all description," according to *Baseball* magazine. Thousands of bells and whistles created a wall of noise. Police chased down the field crashers and restored order.

Shirley was on second and Harris on first when Sam Rice came to the plate. McGraw called in the masterful Art Nehf, who had pitched seven innings the previous day. He got Rice to ground out, ending the inning.

What happened next would have been rejected by Hollywood producers as too shamelessly contrived. Walter Perry Johnson, the man who had been the best thing about the Senators for seventeen years, emerged from the bullpen and headed for the mound to pitch the ninth inning. The Big Train would get one more chance to win a World Series. It was, according to the Senators' historian Tom Devaux, "perhaps the most breathtaking

moment in the history of the Washington Senators; it was perhaps the most breathtaking moment of baseball's illustrious history." Hazel Johnson later recalled:

> [When Walter came out] I saw men crying unashamed, and
> men and women praying aloud. Call it an emotional debauch
> or just a paid performance, as you will. It was more than a
> ballgame to me. It was life and death.

Yet others weren't as thrilled, murmuring that this wasn't the
same Walter Johnson who had come to the Senators in 1907.
Christy Mathewson, the former great Giants pitcher, was skep-
tical. "Poor old Walter, it's a shame to send him in," he said in
the press box. Even funnyman Al Schacht, Johnson's close friend,
had doubts. "I wouldn't have given ten cents for Johnson's
chances when he came in," he said later. "He was tired."

When Johnson got to the mound, Bucky Harris was waiting for him. "You're the best we've got, Walter," he said simply.
"We've got to win or lose with you."

Johnson would later avow that if he "didn't actually pray,"
he was "thinking along those lines." He felt some small relief
that a cloud of cigarette and cigar smoke was settling in Griffith
Stadium. It provided cover. He didn't want to see the faces of
the fans he might disappoint.

Almost no one knew it at that moment, but it was a different Walter Johnson on the mound than the one who had lost
games one and five. Umpire Billy Evans, who had witnessed
Johnson's hand shake nervously before the first game, noticed
the difference when he once again asked him to sign some balls
before game seven. This time, Johnson's hand "as he traced his
signature was as firm and steady as of old." That spirit was also
evident to Clark Griffith: "I never saw such a grim face as Johnson's when Harris gave him the ball," he later said. "He grabbed
the ball so hard the white showed through his knuckles."

As Johnson threw five warm-ups, people began to realize
that the pitcher's celebrated fastball, which had deserted him
in the Series, was back. One witness described the scene: "As
the ball slapped into Ruel's big mitt with the crack of a rifle shot,
the throngs were startled to the realization that the big fellow's

fastball had somehow been restored to him." Bucky Harris said: "When he warmed up I knew he had his stuff."

The first batter Johnson faced was Freddie Lindstrom, who popped out to third base. Next came Frankie Frisch, who had a 1–1 count when he drove a ball deep to the right-field corner. Once again, Griffith's temporary bleachers played a part. Had they not been there, it might have been an inside-the-park home run. As it turned out, the ball bounced off the bleachers, allowing Earl McNeely to chase it down and hurl it back to the infield, holding Frisch to a triple.

The crowd fell silent. Johnson might be about to fail once more.

Ross Youngs came to the plate, according to one witness "swinging his club all the way from the dugout and veritably exuding vengeance at the mighty Johnson." Harris had a long talk with Johnson at the mound and told him to give an intentional walk to Youngs.

There were now men on first and third with one out. Long George Kelly came up to the plate. In the press box, Ty Cobb described his demeanor as "brimful of determination." Johnson wound up and fired a fastball down the middle. Kelly swung and missed. Johnson then fired the same pitch to the same spot, sticking with what made him the greatest pitcher in baseball history, a ball so fast that it could not be hit. Johnson let fly yet another. "The Giant Kelly suddenly found himself facing the Johnson of a decade ago," Grantland Rice would write. "Blinding, baffling speed that struck him out closed down on the rally with a snap of death." Kelly swung and missed.

Yet Washington still had to make the third out. Because of Harris's strategy to keep Bill Terry out of the game, the next batter wasn't Terry, but Irish Meusel. With the count 1–1, Ross Youngs stole second. Ruel didn't even bother to throw to second and risk a run scoring.

Meusel took another ball. He swung on the next pitch, and a gasp went up at Griffith Stadium. The ball had been hit to Ralph Miller at third—hapless, clumsy, frightened Ralph Miller, who was only playing because of Peckinpaugh's injury and whose errors had almost cost Washington the Series. Miller fielded the ball, but his throw to first looked like it was going to be wide.

As Frisch headed for home plate, Joe Judge, the smallest first baseman in baseball, stretched to his limit and snagged Miller's throw for the third out. Frisch hadn't crossed the plate in time. The score remained 3–3.

There was one out in the bottom of the ninth when Judge singled, then moved up to third on an infield hit by Ossie Bluege. McGraw brought in relief pitcher Hugh McQuillan. If the next Senator up could simply get Judge home, the Senators would be world champions. But Ralph Miller promptly hit into a double play. In his last year as a player in 1934, Joe cited this as his most frustrating moment in the major leagues. "Imagine that," he said. "I was only 90 lousy feet from the championship and couldn't make it." The game was going into extra innings.

The Big Train shut New York down in the top of the tenth. Hack Wilson drew a walk, but Travis Jackson struck out and Hank Gowdy hit into a double play. In the bottom half of the inning, Walter Johnson was at the plate with one out when he drove a ball deep into left center. The crowd at Griffith rose as one while the ball looked to be going for a home run. It was just short, Hack Wilson making the catch only ten feet from the fence.

In the eleventh, the Giants once again tried to crack Johnson. Veteran Heinie Groh, pinch-hitting for pitcher Hugh McQuillan, lined a single into right field. Billy Southworth was sent in as a pinch runner at first. The next hitter, Freddie Lindstrom, laid down a sacrifice bunt, sending Southworth to second. Johnson was now facing the heart of the Giants' order. But he fooled Frankie Frisch with a change-up, striking out the Giants' captain, who had struck out only twenty-four times all season.

This brought up Ross Youngs. After a conference at the mound with Harris, Johnson intentionally walked Youngs, putting runners at first and second. Long George Kelly took the first pitch for a strike, then fouled off the second. Johnson threw a high fastball, which Kelly took for a ball. Then Johnson threw a curve, the same pitch that had fanned Frisch. Kelly uncoiled and missed for the third strike.

The fans at Griffith came to their feet and stayed on them as Washington came up in the bottom of the eleventh, but the best the Senators could do was Goose Goslin's short bloop double to right field with two outs. The next batter, Judge, was intentionally walked, bringing up Ossie Bluege, who hit a grounder to shortstop Jackson, who threw to Frisch, forcing Judge out at second.

The Giants led off the twelfth with a single to right by Irish Meusel, but Johnson struck out Hack Wilson and got Jackson and Gowdy on easy outs.

It was at this point that Johnson, as he later described it, began to feel that he and the Senators could not lose this game. "I'd settled down to believing, by then, that maybe this was my day."

In the bottom of the twelfth, Ralph Miller grounded out to start the inning. This brought up Muddy Ruel, who was 0–19 in the Series. Ruel swung at the first pitch, popping it up high and foul behind the plate. It was a playable ball, and Giants catcher Hank Gowdy dropped his mask and drifted back, eyes skyward. Suddenly a breeze blew the ball back towards the plate, and Gowdy adjusted position, moving foward to make the catch. He put his glove up and stepped into his catcher's mask. His foot stuck there. Gowdy shook it like it had fallen asleep, then stumbled. The ball tipped off his glove. As one witness put it, "He caught it—he just didn't squeeze it."

This broken play, at least to one player—and one owner— was a sign that the 1924 Washington Senators were a team of destiny. Freddie Lindstrom later mused, "By that time, I suppose, even an 18-year-old boy like myself, who knew nothing about fate, should have begun to see the light. Washington was supposed to win this game and that's all there was to it." Clark Griffith was also thinking there was some other force at work. "That mask up and bit Gowdy," was the way he put it. "He was going to catch that pop foul and it grabbed it away from him."

Griffith was at a good vantage point to see the Gowdy play up close. In the eighth inning he had moved from his owner's box to a spot near the dugout so he would be in a position to escort President and Mrs. Coolidge from the stadium when—

and however—the game ended. Right after he moved, the Senators had begun to rally. The superstitious Griffith hadn't budged since. He hadn't even sat down.

Given a new life at the plate, Muddy Ruel drove a pitch down the left-field line for a double. Walter Johnson came up. He swung on the first pitch, hitting a grounder to Jackson at shortstop. Acting like he was going to third, Ruel distracted Jackson long enough to allow Johnson to make it to first. One out, two men on.

The shadows were lengthening over Griffith Stadium. Standing at first base, Johnson glanced at the seats. He located his wife and mother, both looking tense. In the press box, Ty Cobb and Babe Ruth shook their fists at him in encouragement.

Earl McNeely, the Senators' fourth batter of the inning, came up. McNeely was a pull hitter, often driving pitches to left field; indeed, McNeely "couldn't hit a ball to right if his life depended on it," according to Al Schacht, who was surprised when John McGraw didn't make a change in the outfield. In the previous inning, McGraw had switched Meusel and Youngs, putting Youngs in left field because he had a superior arm if a right-handed batter got a hit and there was a close play at the plate. But this time McGraw, baseball's mastermind, did nothing.

McNeely fouled off the first pitch. He swung at the second, sending a grounder to Freddie Lindstrom at third. It was an easy double-play ball. Ruel ran hard for third, trying to break it up. He saw Lindstrom, crouching and with his hands at his chest, waiting for the ball.

There are people in Washington, particularly old-timers, who speculate to this day on what happened next. Some say the ball hit a pebble; others think God Himself made it hop. Whatever the reason, the grounder suddenly skipped over Lindstrom's head and landed in left field, and Muddy Ruel, the slowest man on the team, was headed for home. Irish Meusel, not expecting the ball to make it past Lindstrom, had not immediately charged towards the hit. But Ruel was still only halfway to the plate. To Harris, who was on deck, Ruel seemed to move slower the harder he ran. Griffith would later say that watching Ruel heading for home "seemed to last an eternity."

What happened next is another baseball mystery.

Meusel never made the throw. He simply—some say casually—picked up the ball, stuck it in his glove and headed for the dugout.

Muddy Ruel crossed the plate. The Washington Senators were world champions.

"Dante's Inferno at yell-time wasn't in it with the saturnalia of noise [at Griffith Stadium]," reported *Baseball* magazine. Walter Johnson simply stood on second with tears in his eyes, looking towards home. He was probably too shocked to realize that his life might be in jeopardy from people who loved him and were now cascading down from the stands. There was only one exit for the players, through the Washington dugout. Muddy Ruel, the lawyer, had smartly kept running after crossing the plate and made it safely to the dugout. Some players looked like surfers, carried by the wave of fans rolling towards the dugout. The Giants players also, according to Damon Runyon, were "being tossed around in the crowd like bits of driftwood in a running stream."

President Coolidge stood near the exit watching Walter Johnson, who was now attempting to make his way to the clubhouse. Johnson would remember how someone yelled to him, "I'll bet Cal'd like to change places with you right now, Walter." He finally fought his way into the locker room.

Earl McNeely, who had driven in the winning run, was the last man off the field. He had his shirt torn off and only made it into the clubhouse with the help of police.

In the Giants' clubhouse, the players were subdued but not crushed. As Jack Bentley said to Freddie Lindstrom, "Walter Johnson is such a loveable character that the good Lord didn't want to see him get beat again." Meanwhile, a more elaborate summary of what had happened was being written by Heywood Broun of the *New York World:*

> I was never swept by the Easter story until I saw the seventh game of the World Series. I have seen Osiris die in the darkness and come back from his cavern into the sunlight to conquer. Mithras, Adonis, Krishna, Atlas, Hercules—all these I take to be symbols of the human spirit, and so without

incongruity I may add Walter Johnson to the list. To see him throw the ball past the clubs of the Giants was to be consoled with the thought of the might of man and the manner in which he may overcome all the forces of frailty.... The road from the top down to despair is long, but the return may be no more than a night's journey. Every one of us is born again. We die in failure, and out of nothing, out of this very bleakness, we make for ourselves a new morning, a new hope, and a new strength.... When I want to reassure myself that the soul of man is too staunch to die, I will remember that Walter Johnson struck out George Kelly with one out and a runner on third base.

The Senators' locker room was pandemonium. The players shouted, hugged and wandered around in a state of shock. Bucky Harris was so excited he forgot to put his clothes back on after showering. He was shaking hands and slapping backs when Clark Griffith appeared. Griffith hugged Harris, saying, "I'm certainly proud of you, Bucky Boy." Harris became so effusive that trainer Mike Martin advised him to calm down so as to avoid a nervous collapse. "Get away from me, Mike," Harris said. "There's nothing the matter with me. I've just got to blow off some steam." Looking at himself in the mirror as he combed his hair into a perfect part, he was still unaware that he was naked. He managed to put on some clothes before he left the clubhouse.

Walter Johnson just kept repeating to himself: "Gee, I was lucky, wasn't I?"

Several Giants, including John McGraw, dropped by to congratulate the Senators. Then police cleared the way outside the stadium so the players could get through. Some of them headed to a dance at the Willard Hotel, where Commissioner Kenesaw Landis spoke to the cheering throng. "The difference between the two teams could be measured by a hair," he said. Then Landis, the man with the phlegmatic soul and the face of Gibraltar, smiled. "Well," he said, "I suppose it is permitted even the baseball commissioner to feel good that if Washington had to win, Walter Johnson was the pitcher."

Next, Clark Griffith got up:

It is useless to say that this is the happiest moment of my life.
This is the vindication of my judgment. I have always had
faith in Bucky Harris since the first time I saw him. Another
vindication is that I am the only fellow in the world who was
certain that Washington was a baseball town. For twelve years
it's been a long haul.

While Harris and Griffith were being toasted and others
were dancing, there were some who barely had time to cele-
brate. They had made an appointment—to play baseball. In late
September, Al Schacht had set up an off-season exhibition tour
and some of the players had signed up. The first game, a benefit for a crippled elderly man who was going to lose his home,
was scheduled for October 11 in Rochester, New York. So right
after winning the World Series, Johnson, Judge, Nick Altrock
and Al Schacht found themselves trying to get home and catch
a train. "Joe Judge was given a real neighborly welcome home,"
the *Washington Post* reported the next morning. "Hundreds of
fellow residents in the vicinity of Allison Street were waiting
for him to come home, and it was with difficulty that he caught
his train." My aunt Anita, six at the time, always remembered
the commotion outside the house.

There were celebrations all over the city. The *Washington
Post* reported:

> The whirlwind of joy which swept over Washington yester-
> day ... continued to rage until well after midnight. It subsided
> then only because a baseball-crazed city had yelled itself hoarse
> and stopped from sheer exhaustion.... Every one of the more
> than 400,000 men, women and children who make Washing-
> ton their home took part in the celebration. Every noise-mak-
> ing device that hands could reach was used to provide a mighty
> din that continued unchecked for hours.

On Pennsylvania Avenue, the city's main street, the spec-
tacle was, according to a *Post* reporter, almost impossible to
describe. It seemed as if the entire city and "100,000 automobiles" were jammed onto the Boulevard of Base Ball. Newspa-
pers were shredded and dropped as confetti from the office
buildings. On the ground, there were "jams of humanity" that

some feared "might never untangle." The town was "drunk with happiness."

Fred Lieb, the dean of the Baseball Writers Association of America, described the remarkable scene:

> After the last game of the 1924 World Series I was alone with [Commissioner] Landis for a few moments on a little balcony outside his room in the Raleigh Hotel in Washington. Below us on Pennsylvania Avenue snake-danced a joy-maddened crowd. Washington's beloved Senators had just won the deciding seventh game, and Saint Walter Johnson had been the winning pitcher in a 12-inning cliffhanger. Congressmen, department heads, merchants, barbers, bootblacks, janitors, secretaries—all joined in the frivolity. They blew trumpets and beat drums—some beat wash basins with large spoons. Anything that could make noise was being used in this joyous paean of victory. Landis put his hand on my shoulder and looked directly in my eyes as he said, "Freddie, what are we looking at now—could this be the highest point of what we affectionately call our national sport? Greece had its sports and its Olympics; there must have been a year at which they were at their peak. I repeat, Freddie, are we looking at the zenith of baseball?"

TWILIGHT

The Senators went to the World Series two more times after 1924, in 1925 and 1933. The 1925 Series was in many ways as wild and exciting as the 1924 classic.

Walter Johnson was thirty-seven in 1925 and had reconsidered retirement. Griffith acquired two new pitchers in 1925, future Hall of Famer Stan Coveleski and Dutch Ruether. Other players picked up where they had left off the previous season: Goose Goslin hit .334, Sam Rice .350, Joe Judge (now thirty-one) .314, Bucky Harris .323 and Muddy Ruel .310. The Senators would finish second in the majors in fielding. (On May 28, the combination of Peck-to-Harris-to-Judge was responsible for five double plays in one game, a league record.) It didn't hurt the Senators' chances when the Yankees were eliminated from the pennant race due to a season-long "bellyache" suffered by that prodigious eater Babe Ruth, who missed 64 games. (Amusingly, at a critical phase of the 1924 season, the Yankees had lost Ruth for a few hours when the Bambino had a stomachache: he had downed a dozen hotdogs and five sodas during a train stop in Ohio.)

Walter Johnson again pitched brilliantly. He went 20–7, and his 3.07 ERA was the third best in the league. In the World Series the Senators faced the Pittsburgh Pirates. The Pirates had strong pitching and great defense, going 150 games without being shut out, which stood as a record until 1993. They would take advantage of mistakes made by the older Washington team, most conspicuously those made by the American League's Most Valuable Player, Roger Peckinpaugh, who had eight errors in the Series—still a record. Judge had a few key hits, including a home run, but his batting average for the Series was a dismal .174.

The 1925 Series had one of the most controversial plays and oddest finishes of any in history. In the eighth inning of game three, the Senators, playing at home, were in the field and up 4–3. Fred Marberry, pitching in relief, struck out the first two Pirates. The third, catcher Earl Smith, blasted a drive towards the center-right bleachers. Sam Rice raced back for the ball, tumbling into the bleachers just as it hit his mitt. It took him a few seconds to emerge from the crowd with the ball. Pirates manager Bill McKechnie charged out of the dugout and protested that a fan had handed Rice the ball. The four umpires conferred, ruling that Rice had indeed caught it. McKechnie walked over to Commissioner Landis's box and asked if he could appeal. "No," said Landis.

After the game, Landis had a private meeting with Rice. "Sam, did you really catch that ball?" he asked. Rice replied, "The umpire said I did." Landis said that was the answer he wanted Rice to give whenever he was asked about the play. The play—or "The Catch," as many fans and sportswriters came to refer to it—would cause a rule change. After 1925, when an outfielder left the field to go for a ball in the stands, it would be ruled a home run.

Had Sam Rice caught the ball? The answer, for those who choose to believe it, came almost sixty years later. After baseball, Rice started a chicken farm in Ashton, Maryland—Sam Rice's Chicken Hatchery. After contributing eggs to the World War II effort, Rice sold the farm in 1945 and spent his time raising pigeons. On February 9, 1963, eleven days before his seventy-third birthday, he got a call from Cooperstown telling him he had been inducted into the Hall of Fame. He seemed apathetic when asked for a reaction. "If it were a real Hall of Fame," he told reporters, "you'd say Cobb, Speaker, Walter Johnson, Babe Ruth, Lou Gehrig and a few others belonged, and then you'd let your voice soften to a mere whisper." Over time, Rice seemed to appreciate the honor, however. Every year, along with his second wife, Mary, and their daughter, Christine, he would drive up to Cooperstown. On their visit in 1965, Rice told some fellow Hall of Famers that he had written a letter revealing the truth about "the catch," and that it was to be opened after his death.

On October 13, 1974, Rice died of cancer. At a November 5 press conference the letter was read:

> It was a cold and windy day—the right field bleachers were crowded with people in overcoats and wrapped in blankets, the ball was a line drive headed for the bleachers towards right center. I turned slightly to my right and had the ball in view all the way, going at top speed and about 15 feet from bleachers jumped as high as I could and back handed and the ball hit the center of pocket [*sic*] in glove (I had a death grip on it). I hit the ground about 5 feet from a barrier about 4 feet high in front of bleachers with all the brakes on but couldn't stop so I tried to jump it to land in the crowd but my feet hit the barrier about a foot from top and I toppled over on my stomach into first [*sic*] row of bleachers. I hit my Adams apple on something which sort of knocked me out for a few seconds but [Earl] McNeely around that time grabbed me by the shirt and picked me out. I remember trotting back towards the infield still carrying the ball for about half way and then tossed it towards the pitchers mound. (How I have wished many times I had kept it.)
>
> At no time did I lose possession of the ball.
>
> [Signed] "Sam" Rice

The 1925 Series would also witness one of the wildest baseball games ever played. It took place on October 15, 1925. It had rained the entire day before, and Forbes Field in Pittsburgh was a mud hole. Although it was still drizzling and the field was a mess, Commissioner Landis insisted that the game be played. The Series had been delayed twice already, and the forecast called for more rain.

By the fifth inning, it was pouring again and a fog had settled onto the field. In the outfield, Sam Rice could barely make out what was going on in the infield. ("Oh, it was ridiculous," was his comment later.) Ring Lardner wrote that the field "resembled nothing so much as Chicken à la King." James R. Harrison in the *New York Times* was even more colorful:

> [It was] the wettest, weirdest, and wildest game that fifty years of baseball has ever seen. Water, mud, fog, mist, sawdust, fumbles, miffs, wild throws, wild pitches, one near fistfight, impossible rallies—these were mixed up to make the best and worst game of baseball ever played in this country.

Harrison's mention of sawdust refers to attempts made by the grounds crew to dry off the pitcher's mound using sawdust. By the end of the game, one writer noted, Walter Johnson looked as if he were covered in oatmeal.

The Senators were leading 6–4 in the sixth when Commissioner Landis turned to Griffith and told him that he was calling the game. "You're the world champs," he said. But Griffith argued for Landis not to halt play: "Once you've started in the rain you've got to finish it." The commissioner relented. The Pirates staged a comeback, winning the game 9–7 and taking the Series—the first time a team had ever come back from a 3–1 deficit.

☙

AFTER THE 1925 SEASON, the Senators began to lose players from the great World Series rosters. In 1926, Walter Johnson went 15–16, with his worst ERA ever: 3.61. On April 16, 1926—Opening Day— Joe Judge welcomed his third child, Dorothy, into the world. Granddad would hit .291 in the Senators' eighth-place finish.

Johnson hoped to have one great year left in him and signed a one-year contract for 1927. Then his season and his career were ended—by my grandfather. On March 9, the Senators were in spring training camp. Johnson was pitching, and umpire Billy Evans, Bucky Harris and Clark Giffith were all remarking on how well he was throwing.

Then Johnson pitched a ball to Joe Judge, who drove it straight back to the mound, striking Johnson's left ankle.

The Big Train collapsed. Nick Altrock and Al Schacht, thinking the whole thing was a goof, rushed to the mound and

started singing "London Bridge Is Falling Down." Schacht did
a ten-count. As Shirley Povich would later write, Schacht was
unaware that he was "tolling the fatal [ten-count] over the greatest pitching career in major-league history."

Johnson was put in a cast, and stayed home while the team
went on a spring tour. "Words cannot tell you how sorry I am
over your injury," my grandfather wired.

Johnson's career was effectively over. He was uneven all
season. August 2, 1927, marked the twentieth anniversary of his
first start. As he had in his first game, Johnson faced the Detroit
Tigers. He gave up four runs in the fifth and Washington lost
7–6. But tributes were held at Griffith Stadium, and Johnson
was given the day's receipts: $14,476.05. He played in his final
game on September 30, and on October 15 his release from Washington was announced. The Senators finished third, twenty-five
games behind one of the greatest teams of all time, the 1927 New
York Yankees. Johnson would be back in Washington as a manager for four years starting in 1929, but the best his teams would
finish was second.

Walter Johnson still owns a number of baseball records: most
shutouts, fewest home runs allowed in a season, shutouts won on
Opening Day, consecutive seasons with more than three hundred
innings. He is the best ever in shutouts (110) and seasons leading
the league in strikeouts (8), and second only to Cy Young in complete games (531), wins (417). He holds American League records
for total innings, chances, assists, fielding percentage, fewest errors,
and on and on. He was simply the best pitcher who ever lived.

IN FEBRUARY 1928, JOE JUDGE had his fourth child: my father,
Joseph Ralph Judge. He hit .306 and the Senators finished fourth.
That same year Roger Peckinpaugh went to manage the Cleveland Indians, where he would ultimately become president and
general manager. Bucky Harris managed until 1928, when he
was fired after the Senators finished fourth. Harris was thirty-
two at the time, and hit .204 for the season. He had married the
daughter of a West Virginia senator, leading some to speculate
that the sudden immersion into the power elite of Washington

had gone to his head. Be that as it may, Harris would be back as manager of the Senators twice—from 1935 to 1942 and from 1950 to 1954. Griffith always had a soft spot for the man who in spring 1924 had derisively been called "the boy manager."

The Senators finished fifth in 1929 (Judge hit .315). By the mid-1930s, most of the members of the championship Senators were gone. In June of 1930, Goose Goslin was traded to the St. Louis Browns for Heinie Manush, the slugger he had beaten out—thanks to some prompting from Joe Judge—for the batting title in 1928. Goose then went on to Detroit, where he played in two more World Series, in 1934 and 1935. In the 1935 Series he hit a game-winning single in the ninth inning of the final game. The Tigers released him in May of 1938, and he got a call from Clark Griffith. Goose would later describe what happened:

> [Griffith] was a wonderful man, always helpful and kind. He wasn't like a boss, more like a father. He was *more* than a father to me, that man. He called me up after Detroit released me.
>
> "You started with me 18 years ago," he said. "Why don't you come back to Washington and finish up with me?"
>
> So I did. I went back to the Senators for the rest of the season. Didn't play too much, though. Couldn't gallop around in that pasture like I used to 20 years before. Fact is, I didn't even complete my last time at bat. Lefty Grove was pitching against us—he wasn't any spring chicken anymore, either—and I swung at a low outside pitch and wrenched my back.
>
> Bucky Harris was managing Washington again . . . and sent in a pinch-hitter to finish my turn at bat.
>
> "Come on out, Goose," he said, "and rest up a bit."
>
> That was the last time I ever picked up a bat in the big leagues. It was also the first and only time a pinch-hitter was ever put in for the ol' Goose.

Ossie Bluege stayed in Washington, talking over the manager's job from Bucky Harris in 1943. He was manager for five years, his teams finishing in second place in 1943 and 1945.

Fred Marberry was traded to the Tigers in 1930, when the great reliever was thirty-four. By that time his pitching peers from the championship Senators were already gone: Tom Zachary was traded to the Browns in 1926, Curly Ogden sent to the minors in 1925, and George Mogridge packed off to the Browns.

Catcher Muddy Ruel stayed with Washington until 1931, and his love of baseball was so great that he never went back to practicing law—with one minor exception. In 1945, A. B. "Happy" Chandler succeeded Kenesaw Landis as commissioner, and he hired Muddy as a legal advisor. He didn't last very long in this capacity, however, and he returned to the Browns as manager in 1947. He ended up as manager of the Detroit Tigers, retiring in 1961. Muddy Ruel died in 1963, the same year as Joe Judge.

The Senators would achieve one more World Series, in 1933, when they lost to the Giants. That Series brought Sam Rice's last at-bat as a Senator. He was forty-three years old and rarely playing anymore, but was called in to pinch-hit in the seventh inning of game two. Rice's World Series average was .290 before this at-bat, and when he singled to center he raised it to .302. It was another impressive figure in an amazing career: a .322 batting average, 2,987 hits, two years leading the American League in putouts for an outfielder. At age forty, Rice had hit .349 with 73 RBIs; at forty-four, he hit .293 while with the Cleveland Indians, who were then being managed by Walter Johnson.

$$\mathcal{O}$$

BY NOW, GRANDDAD'S TIME AS a ball player was almost over. On June 28, 1930, he received what was then a rare, but now a familiar sign of a career twilight: his own benefit day. Clark Griffith decided to show his appreciation for Judge's fifteen years of service for the Senators by having a Joe Judge Day at the stadium. The Tigers were in town, but agreed to take only $7,000, with the rest of the gate going to Joe. The *Washington Star* reported the next day:

> Now Joe Judge knows how highly esteemed he is by Washington fandom. The fans made his day—Judge Day—yesterday something long to be remembered in Washington baseball history. Teammates praised him, friends showered him with gifts and contending clubs contributed handsomely to the purse presented to the player. It was a big time all around.

After 15,935 fans came through the gates, Joe Judge was presented with a check for $7,447.74. The figure was rounded up to $8,000 when additional gifts and checks were added in. His teammates gave him a silver pitcher and platter. Commander Emmett Doyle of the Eighth Police Precinct offered a handmade divan and cover. Checks came from the mayor of Warrenton, Virginia, and various other admirers from Maryland and Virginia. The Kay Jewelry Company presented a diamond-studded gold wristwatch, and the Continental Baking Company wheeled out a mammoth three-tier cake. My aunt Anita told me that when he brought the cake back to Allison Street, it was too big to fit through the front door.

Along with the gifts and speeches, there was entertainment. Nick Altrock and Al Schacht did one of their celebrated comedy routines, this one reenacting a recent heavyweight fight. And Sylvester Breen, president of a minor league club in Alexandria, Virginia, "donned a dress of an Irish colleen of years ago and danced a reel. There was an eight-year-old acrobatic dancer, and two bands."

Even Joe's father, Joseph Patrick Judge, who had arrived in America from a small farm in Ireland almost fifty years before, had come down from New York for the game. Apparently he still had his brogue, as he told a reporter that he didn't believe anyone could throw a curve ball. " 'Tis impossible," he asserted. "It can't be done."

His son was awed by the attention. "Everyone has treated me so great that it almost overwhelms me," he told the *Washington Post*. "It's been wonderful, so wonderful that I can't think of words to tell you how I feel. I'll never forget this day." He hit two singles and a triple, helping the Senators down Detroit 12–3.

Within a year of Joe Judge Day, my grandfather's career would also effectively come to an end. Walter Johnson had been named manager of the Senators in 1929. He brought them to a fifth-place finish that year and a second-place spot in 1930. Johnson, as close as he was to Joe, had his eye on a 24-year-old first baseman named Joe Kuhel. Johnson thought that Granddad was too prone to injury, and wanted to bring Kuhel up from Baltimore. (There was some speculation that this caused a rift between the two men, but if so, they had a funny way of showing it: in the off season they appeared at a courthouse in Maryland together, applying for hunting licenses.)

Griffith stood with Judge, claiming that the veteran was the better player, at least at bat. The *Washington Star* agreed. The paper made this assessment on April 7, 1931:

> The [Senators] management has been banking on Kuhel to afford Joe Judge the rest periods the veteran is bound to need in the course of the regular campaign, but he hasn't a China-man's chance to horn into the lineup as things stand now. It is held that his RBIs will clear shortly, but at present he is a total flop at bat.

Joe Judge won his spot, and was stationed at first on May 1, 1931, for a game in Boston. He began to feel pain in his stomach in the third inning, and it had gotten so bad by the fifth that he took himself out of the game. He was taken to Peter Bent Brigham Hospital, and at nine o'clock that night they decided to take out his appendix. His physician, Dr. Francis C. Newton, only days before had treated another player, George Herman Ruth, who had injured his thigh.

The Senators immediately sent an aide to Baltimore to retrieve Joe Kuhel. Still, some people held out hope that Judge would quickly come back. One was *Washington Star* sports editor Denman Thompson, who summed up the situation in his "On the Side Lines" column:

> Joe Judge's friends—and there are legions of them throughout baseball as well as in Washington—are intensely gratified that his appendix was so promptly diagnosed and that the required emergency measures proved so eminently successful.
>
> The enforced loafing, for a man of Judge's temperament, and who is accustomed to the daily endeavors entailed by his profession, will constitute as tough an ordeal for him as the actual operation itself.

But there would be no coming back this time. Joe's batting average dropped from .326 in 1930 to .284 in 1931, and to .258

in 1932, when he turned thirty-eight. He still held hopes of being a part of the Senators, this time as manager. In the winter of 1932, he met privately with Clark Griffith to discuss strategies to help Washington win. According to my father, Joe left that meeting believing he was going to be named the next manager, replacing Walter Johnson, who had led the team to third-place finishes in 1931 and 1932.

Granddad was doing some off-season brainstorming in Canada for his next role when he heard the news over the radio: the Senators' new manager would be shortstop Joe Cronin, who happened to be Griffith's new son-in-law. Cronin would lead the team to the World Series, where they lost to the New York Giants, managed by Bill Terry, the slugger whose style Bucky Harris had so effectively cramped in the crucial seventh game of the 1924 triumph.

On Friday at ten o'clock, January 27, 1933, the Washington Senators announced that Joe Judge had been traded to Brooklyn. He was going back to his old neighborhood. He didn't end up playing much with the Dodgers, but he did have one poignant moment. On May 14, 1933, the Phillies were at Ebbets Field. In the eighth inning, with Brooklyn down by two runs, Judge was sent in as a pinch hitter. He drew a walk, then was replaced by a substitute runner. Judge watched the inning end with Brooklyn not scoring, then headed back to the locker room. There he found Hack Wilson, the mighty Giants outfielder he had faced in the 1924 World Series. Wilson was now at the end of his career, too (after hitting 56 home runs in 1930). Having also been traded to the Dodgers, he was feeling sorry for himself.

Judge began changing out of his uniform, but then he heard a cheer go up from the crowd. This is how he described the situation:

> It sounded like the Dodgers were putting on a rally in the bottom of the ninth. I figured they might be needing Hack as a pinch hitter. So I went over to him and told him he wasn't doing himself any good just sitting there and he'd better get himself back on the bench [which Wilson did].
>
> In no time at all it seemed, I heard a great shout go up from the crowd. Then the players came charging into the locker

room, whooping it up and congratulating Wilson as they pumped his hand and thumped him on the shoulders. The first three batters in the last of the ninth had got on base. And Hack, up there as a pinch hitter, had hit one of his longest homers to clear the bases and win the ball game.

There wouldn't be any more moments like that on the ball field for my grandfather. Before the end of the season, the Dodgers had traded him to Boston. His last season, 1934, he played in ten games and batted .333.

Ten days after his release from the Red Sox, Joe was hired as a player-manager for the Baltimore Orioles of the International League. He quit after eight days. Many years later, my father told me that Joe had been growing increasingly disenchanted with some aspects of the game. There was the innovation of night games, which he considered a sop to attract nine-to-fivers who didn't know anything about baseball; and players now had agents, which appalled him; and there was a new reliance on relief pitching, first pioneered by Bucky Harris and Fred Marberry. Salaries were growing for players, though he himself had never made more than $10,000 a year—more than an insurance salesman, but not by much. But there was also an element of personal frustration, since he couldn't see the ball at night as well as he might have wished.

After leaving Baltimore, Joe opened his own restaurant, called Joe Judge's. He also moved the family into a new and larger home in the leafy suburb of Chevy Chase. It was a white, three-story house with a back porch and an azalea garden; it was a long way from the slums of Irish Brooklyn.

It was here on Tennyson Street that my grandmother lived until her death in 1987. I spent every Christmas and Easter there while I was growing up, but we never talked much about baseball or the Senators. I always got the sense that my dad and grandmother felt it was tasteless to brag about a famous relative. There was no shrine to Joe Judge in the house on Tennyson Street—only a few pictures, and rumors of a Senators uniform and baseballs signed by Ty Cobb and Babe Ruth tucked away in an upstairs closet. That was it.

Every Christmas, my grandmother would do the "grab bag," filling a green trash bag with small presents—handkerchiefs, paperback books, records—and we children would all line up and one by one pluck something out. Towards the end of her life she would recite our full names, just to prove she was still sharp. I can still see her delicate French features as she said my name, softly clapping her hands to emphasize each part: Mark, Gauvreau, Judge.

Granddad's restaurant was on Georgia Avenue, not far from the family's old house on Allison Street. But by all accounts he never took much interest in the place. His mind was still on baseball, and in 1937 he finally got to coach, for the Hoyas of Georgetown University. "Great was the joy of the student body," reported the university newspaper, *The Hoya,* "and also the playing squad, when the announcement was made officially.... Under the veteran hand of Joe Judge, Georgetown will surely have a team worthy of its name."

He started with a one-year contract, but he would be there for twenty years. In his first season, the team lost only one game, an exhibition match at Griffith Stadium against the Washington Senators. He became a goodwill representative for the Schlitz beer company, making trips to bars around the D.C. area to promote their product. But there came a time when he began to realize that many people didn't remember him. "He was discouraged," my father once told me. "People just didn't care who he was."

Still, his sense of humor never forsook him. One of his Georgetown players, John Hogan—who became a priest in Maryland—remembered how Joe Judge, the beer representative, caught his players in a bar the night before a big game. "I just hope you boys are drinking Schlitz," he said dryly. He and his teams often had reason to feel lighthearted: he never had a losing season at Georgetown, and he sent players to the majors, including Jim Castiglia, who went to the Phillies, and Art Schult, who joined the Yankees.

During World War II, he was a volunteer at the Pepsi Cola Hospitality Center, where soldiers waited to be shipped overseas. Joe regaled them with baseball stories while they downed hotdogs and sodas—for some of them, of course, their last. It was doubtless more inspiring to hear about the Senators of old than the new ones, who from the 1930s through the war performed in the shadow of the Yankees dynasty and often found themselves in the Second Division of the American League.

☙

IN MARCH OF 1946, WALTER JOHNSON was at his Maryland home when he felt a strange numbness in his left arm. A couple of weeks later he needed help cutting a steak. On April 9, Johnson was taken to Georgetown University hospital, where he was diagnosed with a hemorrhage due to a brain tumor and given only days to live.

Clark Griffith immediately came to his bedside, where the two men exchanged stories of past adventures. Johnson went downhill rapidly, and soon was paralyzed along his entire left side; he began to lose his ability to speak. "It breaks your heart to see him lying there," his old teammate Ossie Bluege said, "knowing there isn't a thing in the world you can do for him except to sit with him as long as the nurses will allow."

When Johnson fell into a coma, Griffith held his hand and continued to talk to him. Every day he brought a single rose to the hospital from the rose garden he had started at home using dirt from the Griffith Stadium pitcher's mound. He told a physician, "I felt that anything enriched by Walter's sweat was semi-sacred."

On September 21, 1946, Griffith held a testimonial evening for Walter Johnson at the stadium. Some twenty-four thousand fans showed up, helping to push the Senators' yearly attendance over the one-million mark, the only time in its history the team attracted so many followers. A check for $5,000 was given to help the Johnson family defray the hospital costs, which Clark Griffith would soon assume. After spending his retirement years on a farm in Maryland, the Big Train couldn't afford the bills.

He died on Tuesday, December 10. His nurse, Daisy Barnwell Jones, wrote later that at the moment of his passing, the bustling city of Washington seemed to grow silent:

Mr. Johnson died like he lived—with quiet dignity. Heaven and earth stood in awesome silence at his passing. The ever-present streetcar forever tearing around the corner like a freight train was behind schedule—strangely missing. Not one car passed by, not one voice was heard, save for the noisy press down that hall. The night supervisor, a saintly Sister in long black garb, making her usual rounds, looked in upon the death scene, heard the voices of the press, picked up the phone on the desk just outside Mr. Johnson's room and whispered, "We hear you." With that, all was silent, in the halls, on the street, in his room, everywhere. As gently as a feather wafted out the window. And just as silently, his soul took its flight.

On December 13, 1946, it was a clear and cold December morning in Washington, when a group of the 1924 Senators stood around a seated Clark Griffith in his office at Griffith Stadium.

The men had come together again to bury Walter Johnson. Muddy Ruel, Joe Judge, Bucky Harris, Roger Peckinpaugh and Ossie Bluege, Clyde Milan and Tom Zachary—they were there. A devastated Clark Griffith, "the Moses of Washington baseball," had been giving an interview to Bob Adie of the *Washington Times-Herald.* Adie wrote:

> The energy seemed to be drained out of Griffith. He looked like the outline of a tree in mid-winter, and the twin peaks of snowy eyebrows that have snapped and wagged so furiously in all the old gentleman's bouts down through the years now seemed to hang lank and limp. Those keen old eyes always throwing off sparks like a smithy's forge looked glazed and tired. Occasionally they would puddle up when Griff kept recalling those precious moments with his friend who was gone.

Clyde Milan spoke about Johnson's humility, his unflagging decency. Others told their own stories about him. Joe Judge, talking with the *Washington Post*'s Shirley Povich, described a game in Cleveland when Johnson struck out three batters on nine pitches. And he told a story about rooming with Johnson in St. Louis. They went out to dinner, and towards the end of the meal they decided to take in a movie. As they were leaving the restaurant, Johnson was stopped by a fan. Judge politely stood a few yards away to let the two men talk—watching with growing impatience as Johnson took fifteen minutes with the fan. By the time they got away, Joe was understandably irritated. "We might not make the last show now," he complained. "What on earth were you talking about for so long?"

"This fellow said he was from Kansas," Johnson said. "He was asking about my sister. I had to be nice to him."

Puzzled, Joe said that he didn't know Johnson had a sister.

"I don't," Johnson said. "But I still had to be nice to him."

In his column in the *Post*, Povich offered his own anecdote. After Johnson had retired, he and Povich went to Griffith Stadium to see a pitching sensation named Bob Feller, who was being called "the new Johnson." They watched him with admiration, and afterwards Povich asked Johnson if, in his day, he had thrown faster than Feller. This caused, in Povich's phrase, "a head-on clash of Big Barney's native modesty and his innate honesty." The honesty finally won out. Johnson grinned and said, "I guess I used to throw that thing harder."

Johnson was buried on a hillside in Rockville Union Cemetery in Rockville, Maryland. His procession from the National Cathedral, where the service was held, to the gravesite tied up traffic for a mile on Wisconsin Avenue. Povich described the crowd at the cemetery:

> Bareheaded hundreds, high personalities of the baseball realm, notables of Washington civic life and the peanut vendors who knew the great pitcher at Griffith Stadium, stood in saddened clusters with Johnson's family at the brief gravesite services.

⚾

THE 1950S BROUGHT TELEVISION to the country, and this was a great comfort to my grandfather. He could now watch games at home instead of driving to the stadium, where he would still feel the urge to take the field. He was now approaching sixty, and my father told me that he spent a lot of time watching the games on TV and talking back to the set, arguing about botched plays, giving advice, cursing bad calls. He looked, my father once told me, just like the old man in the movie *Damn Yankees,* trying to push the Senators to victory by yelling at his TV set.

It's an appealing comparison. In 1954 a young journalist, Douglass Wallop, published a book called *The Year the Yankees Lost the Pennant.* After a change of titles, it became the book, then the play, then the film *Damn Yankees.* The hero, Joe Hardy, is an old Senators fan so devoted to the club that he makes a deal with the devil; he'll sell his soul if the devil will make the Senators win the pennant. The devil takes him on, transforming him into an unstoppable young player for Washington. The team wins, but Hardy pays a terrible price and ultimately—no surprise here—has a change of mind.

It is likely that Joe Hardy was based on my grandfather. As a young man in the late 1940s, Douglass Wallop dated Joe Judge's daughter, my Aunt Dorothy. She recalls that Wallop "was steeped in Senators history," spending hours at the house in Chevy Chase exchanging stories with Joe. While she doesn't think Joe Judge was the actual model for Joe Hardy, my father always felt differently: he thought there could be no question about it.

In the movie, Joe Hardy lives in Chevy Chase. As the story begins, we see him sitting in his living room and talking back to the Senators, ghostly figures on his flickering television screen, grousing about their lousy fielding and giving them tips on how to play the game—indeed, doing what Joe Judge was doing when Wallop used to come over to the house.

"That man was my father," Dad used to say whenever the movie was on TV. (Oddly, the devil in *Damn Yankees* stipulates September 24—my birthday—as the day Hardy must relinquish his soul in exchange for becoming a baseball superstar.)

⚬

PERHAPS THE FINAL END OF the classic Senators—and the beginning of the end of the team as a franchise—came on Thursday, October 27, 1955. At 8:40 that night, Clark Griffith died. He had been suffering from cancer and had been admitted to a hospital with a stomach hemorrhage. Doctors frankly told the press and family that due to Griffith's age, eighty-five, it was only a matter of time. Still, the Old Fox was a fighter until the end, as a visiting doctor described him:

> I walked into his room expecting to see a tired, worn man of 85 lying pale, with eyes closed like so many who do surrender to the ordeal of hemorrhage and pain. Instead I was surprised to see Mr. Griffith, with his head propped on a pillow, looking out at me with eyes that were glittering beneath those bushy brows and his lips clenched in a thin straight line. It was a face full of fight and determination. It was a thrill to see the man giving it such a tremendous battle.

Griffith died when the Senators' fortunes were at a low ebb. Just the year before, the team had registered its lowest day of attendance in history: 460 on September 7, 1954, against the Philadelphia Athletics. After Griffith's death, his nephew Calvin took over the franchise, revealing that this uncle had left only $25,000 in the team account. Senators historian Tom Devaux accurately summed up the situation: "More money was being made from concessions and renting Griffith Stadium to football's Redskins than from actual attendance at ballgames. The team had fallen into last place, and Damn Yankees was every Washington Senators fan's nightmare."

Faced with this, the younger Griffith made a series of moves, all of them bad. He struck a nine-player trade with the Red Sox, and all of the players that came to Washington bombed. Then he decided that if he didn't have players who could bring some game to the stadium, he would bring the stadium to them. Before the 1956 season, he had a six-foot screen installed in left field to cut down the distance of a home run from 400 to 350 feet. It did make batting stronger—for opposing teams. The Senators gave up 99 home runs in 1955; in 1956, after the new fence, the number jumped to 171.

My grandfather watched all this with dismay. In his personal life he also suffered a devastating loss. His firstborn, Catherine, died of cancer on July 5, 1957, at age forty-one. She had worked for most of her life as a congressional secretary on Capitol Hill. She and my grandfather used to spend hours sitting around the dinner table, talking politics (both were Democrats), and when she died he was heartbroken. He had just gotten into his car, parked on the hillside street where his daughter Dorothy lived, when he heard the news; he went into shock and his foot came off the brake. Family members had to run and stop the car before it rolled down the hill and crashed.

The next blow came a year later. In August 1958 he was informed by Georgetown that they had a mandatory retirement policy at sixty-five, and he would reach that age on May 25, 1959. "My relationships with the university have been a source of great pleasure to me throughout the years," he wrote in his letter of resignation. "It is with a feeling of sadness that I face their termination." Father Edward Bunin, the president of the university, wrote him back: "It is with equal regret that I accept your decision to retire.... I have been here ten years and attended more baseball games than any other form of sport. I was always impressed by the high quality of your activity and relationship with the students." My Aunt Anita and my father both told me this was a devastating loss. "I always thought that maybe he loved baseball too much," Anita said. "He put his whole heart and soul into the game, and when it was gone he had nothing else." It wasn't long afterward that he began to suffer from diabetes.

Before he retired, Joe was inducted into the Georgetown Hall of Fame, but he has never been admitted into Cooperstown. This might have had something to do with an article he pub-lished in 1959, four years before his death. It has long been an open secret in the family that the article was actually written by my father, who at the time was working for *Life* magazine. Called "Verdict Against the Hall of Fame," it was published in the June 6, 1959 issue of *Sports Illustrated*. It argued strenuously that the Hall of Fame was letting in players who didn't deserve to be there. "The Hall has lost some of its meaning and much of its glory in recent years," it read. My grandfather—or rather my father—named players who were in the Hall for inappropriate reasons. Players Joe Tinker, Johnny Evers and Frank Chance were in simply because of the ring of their double-play combination, Tinkers-to-Evers-to-Chance. Tinkers's lifetime average is .264; Evers's is .270. The article pointed to catcher Ray Schalk, lifetime average .253, and shortstop Rabbit Maranville, who never hit over .300. The essay then blasted the growing tendency to favor players with more personality than talent:

> To be a credit to the game of baseball, a man need not have got off a record number of wisecracks or assembled a record number of feature stories. There are a lot of colorful palookas.
>
> In my day, by the time the infield was finished with spitting tobacco juice and licorice and rubbing the ball down with mud, especially on a dark afternoon, the ball would come at you looking like a clump of coal. A great hitter would lay the wood on it regardless of the side it was thrown from or the stuff on it. That same man could steal the base that made the difference. He was fast enough so that the hit-and-run and bunt-and-run were always possible. And when he got back to his position he could come up with the great catch, the great save, the great throw that meant winning instead of losing.
>
> Today many so-called sluggers couldn't steal a base if they were alone in the park. They are not expected to throw too well or run too fast as long as they can belt the ball out of the park when their one moment of usefulness arrives. The idea of being a team member sometimes is lost completely, and what we have is an association of specialist businessmen investing their specific talents and carefully watching their own special interests. . . .

My grandfather died after suffering a heart attack while shoveling snow on March 11, 1963. The papers reported the news, calling him "the greatest of all the Senators' first basemen." Columnist George Clifford of the *Washington Daily News* summed him up this way: "Judge was not a character in the clownish, bittersweet fashion of sports. The stories about him become legends simply because of his ability."

He played in over 2,000 games, scored more than 1,000 runs, hit safely more than 2,000 times, hit 400 doubles and 150 triples. He held the record for assists by a first baseman, 1,284, until 1955. He led the American League in fielding six times, a first baseman's record he still shares with Don Mattingly. Seventy years after his last season, Joe Judge is still in the top ten in half a dozen categories for fielding. The statistic that still floors me is his .993 fielding average, a league record for thirty years. Joe Judge played in the time when first basemen wore tarps instead of mitts. He was virtually perfect around the bag when it really meant something.

Ossie Bluege, Granddad's old teammate, was unstinting in his praise when he heard of his death. He told the *Boston American,*

> He was the best first baseman in the league in the 1920s, and I'm not forgetting that Lou Gehrig was with the Yankees at the time. Judge could outrun and outfield Gehrig. He was superior on the 3-6-3 double play. He could steal a base when needed, and he could hit in the clutch. The only reason he's not in the Hall of Fame is that he didn't hit the long ball. But I doubt if ever a home run hitter was more valuable to a club.

Boston sportswriter John Drohan backed up Bluege. "Judge used to beat the Red Sox [of the 1920s] more than any other player in the league. And fielding! He was an artist, so unlike the sluggers."

Perhaps the best line summing up Joe Judge came from Sam Rice; when he learned of Joe's death, he said simply, "There was no play he couldn't make."

⚾

AT THE TIME OF JUDGE'S death, Washington had already lost one baseball team when the original Washington Senators were moved to Minnesota in 1960. It was difficult to fault Calvin Griffith for moving the team. The Senators had not finished higher than fourth since the Second World War. Attendance was under half a million every year. Worse, Griffith Stadium itself was in horrible shape. The park was over fifty years old, and it showed. On April 21, 1957, a game was called due to a power failure — a first in major league baseball. (The funniest outage at Griffith had occurred a few years earlier, in a game against the Tigers. The Senators' pitcher was in a windup when the lights suddenly went out. When they came back on a few seconds later, everyone, including the umpires, was face down on the field. No one knew if the pitch had been delivered.)

On top of all that, Griffith could move the team knowing that Washington would not be without a team. On October 26, 1960, American League owners met in New York and agreed on expanding the league to ten teams. What became known as "the original" Senators were out. A new Senators team, owned by an investment group, was in.

It would last ten years. In 1962, the Senators played their last game at Griffith Stadium—attendance 1,498—before moving to D.C. Stadium, which was later renamed Robert Francis Kennedy Stadium, the place where Joe Judge would eventually go up in the Ring of Stars. The site of the old Griffith Stadium became Howard University Hospital. Most of the newly incarnated Senators' final ten years were spent in the cellar, with the exception of a fifth-place finish in 1971.

Most Washingtonians agree that the main villain in the story of the expansion Senators was Robert E. Short, a multimillionaire trucking magnate and treasurer of the Democratic National Committee. In 1969 he bought a majority share in the new franchise, and within two days of the announcement he told the *Washington Star* that he wasn't going to make any promises about keeping baseball in the city. A month later, he announced that if he didn't get certain broadcast and box office revenues, then he would consider taking the team elsewhere. Short, who traveled in a $700,000 Lear Jet, fired Senators manager Jim Lemon and general manager Ed Doherty. He raised ticket prices; at $6.00, a seat in RFK was the most expensive in the majors.

For his new manager, Short acquired baseball legend Ted Williams. He paid Williams $100,000 a year, which came with a $15,000-a-year apartment in Washington and the option to buy 10 percent of the club if he so wished. When Williams signed his contract in February 1969, Short had a news conference and unveiled the new slogan: "It's a Whole New Ballgame."

Over the next two years, the Senators finished fourth and sixth, an improvement over previous seasons. They owed most of their success to Frank "Hondo" Howard, a hitter who bridges the gap between Babe Ruth and Mark McGwire. Howard was 6'7" and over 260 pounds; he routinely sent balls into the bleachers of RFK, inspiring fans to paint the seats yellow where a ball had landed. Howard had been traded to Washington by Los Angeles in 1964, and he quickly made Washington his home.

It was during the Hondo years that I saw my first, and only, Senators game. My father would take my two older brothers to the games every summer, but I was deemed too young to last a full nine innings at RFK. Then, in the summer of 1970, the magic day arrived; I was almost six years old, mature enough not to start squirming after a few innings.

I can remember only a few things about the game. One was how exquisite, how magical, baseball is when it's seen live. In live baseball, there always seems to be something happening even when there isn't. My father showed me something you just don't get from narrow televised images: players adjusting their positions depending on who was up at bat. I was amazed when a left-handed hitter came up and the entire field shifted. And when someone made a hit, you could watch the field move hither and thither, the players interacting as though in a fully staged ballet.

RFK seemed as large as a planet to me. Like most Washington fans, I was mesmerized by Frank Howard, who seemed like a character out of the Marvel comics I read growing up. That day, my brothers tried to figure out how many of me it would take to make a Howard; the final tally, I think, was four. (I only remember a few details of the game—we played the Twins and beat them in the ninth inning, and an ambulance had to come when a foul ball hit a girl in the face, breaking her nose.)

Even epic-sized Frank Howard, however, couldn't save the expansion Senators from Bob Short. Problems with the stadium authority and pleas of poverty led Short to announce, in September 1971, that he, with the approval of a majority of the owners, was moving the Washington Senators to Texas, where they would become the Texas Rangers. Short claimed that Washington just didn't support the team and that the D.C. stadium authority was charging him too much rent on use of RFK. The media's reaction was immediate, with a television sportscaster calling Short "a fink" on the air and an aging Shirley Povich bemoaning in the *Washington Post:*

They won't hear it in Washington next spring when the cry throughout the rest of the land is the joyful sound of "Play Ball," the command that remobilizes a million dreams of pennants, however fanciful. After 71 years, the vacuum and the stillness. The Washington Senators are no more.

As if to emphasize the fact that Washington baseball was fading, in 1971 Goose Goslin died at the age of seventy. He had run a boat rental company on the Delaware Bay after retiring. Goose's career batting average was .316; he had 2,735 hits, more than Lou Gehrig and Joe DiMaggio; he had 500 doubles; his 1,609 RBIs surpassed Tris Speaker and Rogers Hornsby. Three days after his death, Heinie Manush, his rival for the 1928 batting crown, also passed away.

Regarding the end of the Senators, the *Washington Star*, which had provided such wonderful coverage of the team during its heyday in the 1920s, offered what was probably the best editorial, echoing the feelings of many in the city:

> Well, to hell with it. Who needs baseball? It had been particularly dumb in Washington. The only question, through these generations of seasons: Whether we could escape the cellar. Good riddance.
>
> And yet . . . it *was* a thrill to sit in the early spring sunshine at the opening game, eating peanuts while the president threw out the first ball and new hopes sprang eternal, like crocuses. It was good to feel, on that one day, that all eyes were on us as we took part in a ritual every bit as meaningful to millions of Americans as, say, an inauguration.
>
> Washington will keep its inaugurations; it is still, in many ways, the capital of the world. We do not need a baseball team to secure our credentials as a city. We have the White House and the Capitol, and the great men in them. We have our shaded avenues and illuminated monuments. We have a fine new cultural center [the Kennedy Center]. What is Abner Doubleday's somewhat ridiculous game, that we should weep for it?
>
> And yet . . . it *was* good to drive to the stadium through the warmth of a summer evening—to watch the pitcher warming up in front of the dugout—to sing the Star Spangled Banner—

to leap from our seats at the crack of bat on ball—to yell "Charge!" when Frank Howard came to the plate—to drink a beer—occasionally to win. It was good even to watch our boys on TV, carrying the tattered flag to rival cities, brave in defeat, glorious in victory.

Bob Short was not worthy of us, the long-suffering Senator fans. He knew nothing about running a baseball team, and would not leave the job to those who did know. He spent too much, cared too little, and thought he could buy his way out of his mistakes with high-priced tickets. . . . He deserves Texas, and vice versa. Let him go.

And yet . . . it *would* have been nice to see how things developed next year. Was that the ghost of Walter Johnson that walked the mound with young Pete Broberg? Would Jeff Burroughs develop into another Goose Goslin? Someday, all those prospects in our new farm system might have brought a golden era to the city which has waited so long. Who knows?

ON THURSDAY, SEPTEMBER 30, 1971, almost twenty thousand fans came to RFK for the last game of professional baseball in Washington. The Senators were playing the Yankees, but now Babe Ruth's old line from the 1924 pennant race when his team lost out on the last day of the season applied to Washington rather than New York: "You ain't sleeping, boys, you're dead." The decks of the stadium were filled with signs denouncing the man who had stolen their team: "Short Stinks," "Short Changed," and one sign recommending that Short stop in Hell on his way to Texas.

Again, veteran *Washington Post* baseball writer Shirley Povich captured the mood:

> Everybody in Kennedy Stadium stood up at 7:30 P.M. because the voice on the loudspeaker said: "We ask you to join Robert Merrill in singing the National Anthem." The voice did not bother to explain that Merrill was on wax, and that Robert, baby, was not deserting the Metropolitan Opera stage for the occasion. It was merely one more of management's deceptions

Senators fans had long been taught to live with. To those among the crowd who had come in sorrow, the Star Spangled Banner never before sounded so much like a dirge. Francis Scott Key, if he had taken another peek by the dawn's early light, would have seen that the flag ain't still there, and lyricized accordingly. It was captured and in transit to Arlington, Tex., which, to embittered Washington fans, is some jerk town with the single boast it is equidistant from Dallas and Fort Worth.

My older brother Joe wanted to go to the game, but my father was too distraught. Years later my mother told me that, out of sight of the rest of us, he had wept to himself. He almost didn't make it to a business meeting that night.

He missed a home run by Frank Howard, thanks to a fat pitch delivered by Mike Kekich, who more or less conceded after the game that he presented Hondo with a gift because he "felt sorry for the fans." But the fans weren't so easily placated; the Senators were leading 7–5 in the ninth when what one witness described as "the ugly mood" in the stadium boiled over and the spectators stormed the field, forcing the Senators to forfeit the game.

One of the witnesses at the game was Bucky Harris. When the Senators were sold, Harris declined to comment, merely saying that he wanted to "avoid controversy." But as the curtain went down at RFK, Harris was too moved to stay altogether silent. "I just can't believe my eyes," he said. "I never thought I'd see the day when there was no baseball in Washington." He died in 1977, three years after Sam Rice.

WASHINGTON SUPPORTS A MEDIOCRE hockey team, a women's basketball team and the Washington Wizards, perennial NBA second-raters. But, as I write this, there is still no baseball here, though we continue to exchange hopeful rumors that the city of the Swampoodle Grounds and Griffith Stadium, of Ed Delahanty and the Big Train, will again hear the crack of the bat on some sultry summer's night. Surely we would welcome back a team.

It's a shame they won't be able to play where the old Griffith Stadium was, but at least it's a hospital that stands there and not a football or soccer stadium. Knowing what baseball once did for this city, I've always thought it appropriate that the site has become a place of healing.

Index